Gideon v. Wainwright:

THE RIGHT TO FREE COUNSEL

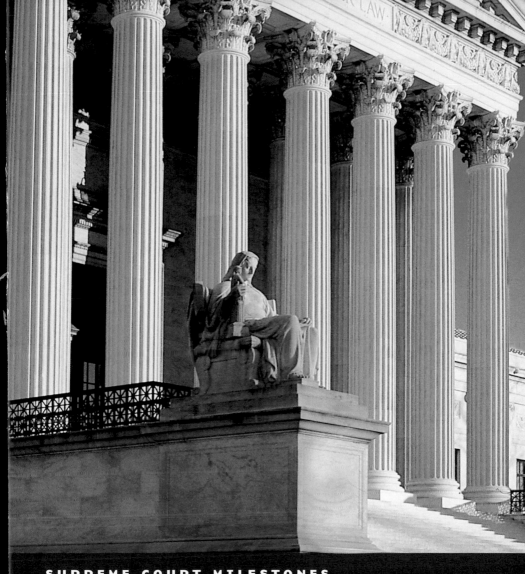

SUPREME COURT MILESTONES

Gideon v. Wainwright:
THE RIGHT TO FREE COUNSEL

RON FRIDELL

Marshall Cavendish
Benchmark
New York

*With special thanks to Professor David M. O'Brien of the
Woodrow Wilson Department of Politics at the University of
Virginia for reviewing the text of this book.*

Marshall Cavendish Benchmark
99 White Plains Road
Tarrytown, NY 10591
www.marshallcavendish.us

All Internet sites were available and accurate when sent to press.
Fridell, Ron.
Gideon v. Wainwright : the right to free counsel / by Ron Fridell.
p. cm. — (Supreme Court milestones)
Includes bibliographical references and index.
ISBN-13: 978-0-7614-2146-7 (alk. paper)
ISBN-10: 0-7614-2146-7 (alk. paper)
1. United States. Supreme Court. [1. Gideon, Clarence Earl—Trials, litigation, etc. 2.
Wainwright, Louie L.—Trials, litigation, etc. 3. Right to counsel—United States.] I.
Title: Gideon versus Wainwright. II. Title.
III. Series.
KF228.G53F75 2006
345.73'056—dc22   2006002803

Photo research by Candlepants Incorporated

Cover Photo: Index Stock Royalty-Free

The photographs in this book are used by permission and through the courtesy of:
Florida State Archives: 6, 29. *National Archives and Records Administration:* 10, 33. *The
Perot Foundation: 35. Corbis:* Bettmann, 22, 41, 89, 92,99, 122. *Getty Images:* Time Life
Pictures, 49, 77; Hulton Archive, 107. *Bruce Jacob:* 65. *AP/Wide World Photos:* 111, 123.
Flip Schulke: 120.

Editorial Director: Michelle Bisson
Art Director: Anahid Hamparian
Series Designer: Sonia Chaghatzbanian

Printed in China
1 3 5 6 4 2

CONTENTS

Cell Inspection 1951

PRISON OFFICIALS INSPECT CELLS IN THE FLORIDA STATE PRISON IN RAIFORD,
WHERE CLARENCE EARL GIDEON WAS LATER HELD AFTER HIS 1961 ARREST.

INTRODUCTION

IT ALL STARTED IN THE EARLY MORNING hours of June 3, 1961. That's when someone broke into a poolroom in Bay Harbor, a sleepy little community in Panama City, Florida. The burglar pried open a cigarette machine and a jukebox and pocketed the cash inside. He stole some wine and might have taken some cigarettes as well.

As burglaries go it doesn't sound like much, and it wasn't. The thief made off with less than one hundred dollars profit for his morning's work. According to Section 811.021 of the Florida Statutes, stealing less than a hundred dollars amounts to petty larceny.

Petty is another way of saying "small," a small crime. But petty larceny is a far more severe offense than the name suggests. In the state of Florida, it's a felony, like murder, rape, and arson. Petty larceny can saddle a convicted defendant with serious jail time, especially if he has served time before.

This was the fearful future facing Clarence Earl Gideon when he was charged with the Bay Harbor poolroom break-in. Gideon had already served four prison terms for burglary, and a fifth conviction could earn him a stiff sentence.

And that's just what happened. Gideon was indigent— he was poor. He did not have the money to hire a lawyer, so he asked the court to appoint a defense attorney for him free of charge.

State courts often granted such requests. But the trial judge said no, so Gideon had to act as his own defense lawyer. The trial took less than a day to complete, the jury took less than an hour to convict, and the judge handed down the maximum sentence: five years in a Florida prison.

But then a series of extraordinary events took place, and two years later the United States Supreme Court reversed Gideon's conviction. Then, for a second time, the state of Florida tried Gideon for the poolroom burglary, and this time he was found not guilty. So after serving two years in prison for a crime he did not commit, Clarence Earl Gideon earned back his freedom.

In between the two trials, an intricate legal drama known as *Gideon* v. *Wainwright* played out, and judicial history was made. Clarence Earl Gideon, a drifter and small-time thief, stood at the center of the action, along with some of the most influential people in the nation. Lawyers, judges, state attorneys general, and state and national lawmakers all played a part. And so did the nation's most powerful team of judges: the nine justices of the United States Supreme Court.

Gideon v. *Wainwright* focused on a glaring flaw in the U.S. criminal justice system: State courts did not have to appoint lawyers free of charge for indigent defendants in criminal trials. So if the court denied him a lawyer, a defendant without means such as Gideon was virtually helpless. Whether innocent or guilty of the crime, he was all but certain to lose in court.

The U.S. Supreme Court ruling in *Gideon* v. *Wainwright* promised to correct that flaw by guaranteeing a defendant's right to counsel. No indigent defendant would ever again be tried in a criminal court without the right to a lawyer to defend him.

Later, Gideon's story would be told in a 1980 made-for-TV movie, *Gideon's Trumpet*. Henry Fonda, an actor well-known and admired for playing American heroes such as Wild West lawman Wyatt Earp, World War II general Douglas MacArthur, and President Abraham Lincoln, would play the role of Clarence Earl Gideon.

Gideon himself would come to be seen as a true American hero: a righteous and determined man who struggled against long odds to regain his precious freedom. And others would benefit from his struggles as well. In the years to come, other indigent defendants would keep their freedom thanks to *Gideon* v. *Wainwright*.

But the struggle did not end with Gideon's judicial victory. It continues today as lawyers and lawmakers continue to fight for the right of indigent defendants to be adequately represented in the nation's criminal courts.

In The Supreme Court of The United States
Washington D.C.

Clarence Earl Gideon
        Petitioner

vs.

H.G. Cochran, Jr., as
Director, Divisions
of corrections state
of Florida

Petition for a writ
of Certiorari Directed
to The Supreme Court
State of Florida.

No. 890 Misc.

OCT. TERM 1961
U. S. Supreme Court

To: The Honorable Earl Warren, Chief
    Justice of the United States
        Comes now the petitioner, Clarence
Earl Gideon, a citizen of The United States
of America, in proper person, and appearing
as his own counsel. Who petitions this
Honorable Court for a Writ of Certiorari
directed to The Supreme Court of The State
of Florida. To review the order and Judge-
ment of the court below denying The
petitioner a writ of Habeus Corpus.
        Petitioner submits That The Supreme
Court of The United States has The authority
and jurisdiction to review the final Judge-
ment of The Supreme Court of The State
of Florida The highest court of The State
Under sec. 344 (B) Title 28 U.S.C.A. and
Because The "Due process clause" of the

GIDEON'S HANDWRITTEN WRIT OF CERTIORARI

one
How It All Began

THE STRUGGLE BEGAN with a large envelope stuffed full of legal documents. Since this was a legal struggle, it was fought with words and ideas rather than physical weapons. But it was an intense struggle for freedom nonetheless.

The envelope was from Clarence Earl Gideon, an inmate of the Florida State Prison in Raiford, Florida. It was addressed to the United States Supreme Court in Washington, D.C. Inside were three legal documents.

GIDEON'S WRIT OF CERT

One was a writ of *certiorari*, or *cert* for short. A cert is a petition of appeal in a civil or criminal case. This cert involved a criminal case. It came from a prisoner, Gideon, who claimed that he was wrongly convicted of a crime. Gideon's writ asked the U.S. Supreme Court to review his case and reverse the conviction.

If the prisoner's appeal succeeds, he is no longer held to be guilty of the crime. But the lower court may choose to try him for that same crime again. Trying a person for the same crime is known as double jeopardy, and the Fifth Amendment to the Constitution forbids it. But when the Supreme Court reverses an appealed conviction, it's as though the original trial never took place at all. The prisoner is back to square one, accused of the crime and awaiting trial. This is the spot where Gideon was hoping to end up. Then he would have to find a way to persuade a second jury that he was not guilty.

Like other legal documents, the cert was supposed to follow certain rules. Gideon's cert violated some of these rules. He had sent only a single copy written by hand in pencil on lined sheets of paper, when the Court said that the cert should be typewritten whenever possible and forty copies should be submitted. Gideon violated another Court rule by not enclosing the filing fee of one hundred dollars. Finally, his petition contained errors in grammar and spelling, which the Court did not like to see in a formal legal document.

At this point it looked as though Gideon's petition might be set aside and never seen by the justices. But on the cert's first page, these words appeared: "Petition for Leave to Proceed in Forma Pauperis." This legal language asks the Court to make an exception to the rules because the prisoner is indigent.

The Court recognizes that many prisoners are indigent and not well educated, and sees to it that these prisoners retain the right to appeal. So Gideon's one-hundred-dollar fee was forgiven, and the Court had the writ typewritten and copied, with Gideon's errors in grammar and spelling intact.

HABEAS CORPUS

The other two documents in the envelope had to do with *habeas corpus*. This Latin phrase means "you have the body." The body, in this case, was Gideon's, imprisoned in the Florida State Prison.

One document was the writ of habeas corpus that Gideon had sent to the Florida State Supreme Court, the highest court in that state. The writ requested that a state appeals court review his case to decide whether he had

appeals courts versus trial courts

Gideon was tried, convicted, and sentenced to prison in a Florida state trial court. He then appealed his conviction to a Florida state appeals court, hoping to have the conviction reversed.

Each state has its own system of appeals courts, with a state supreme court at the top and one or more lower courts below. Appeals courts are different from trial courts. They do not use a judge or jury to determine a defendant's guilt or innocence, as trial courts do.

Instead, a panel of appeals court judges reviews a written record of the original trial with these questions in mind: Was the trial conducted properly, according to the rules of law? Was the decision fair, based on the evidence presented? Were all parties treated fairly? Were anyone's constitutional rights violated? And if so, were these violations serious enough to justify reversing the trial court verdict?

If the answer to the final question is yes, the court will reverse the conviction and send the case back to the trial court. Then it's up to the state to decide whether to re-try the case.

been unlawfully convicted and should be released from prison.

The other document was a reply to that writ of habeas corpus from the Florida Supreme Court. The court felt that Gideon's trial had been properly and fairly conducted and that his conviction and sentence should stand.

This left Gideon with one final chance at getting his conviction reversed. That last chance now lay in the hands of the U.S. Supreme Court, the highest court in the land, in the form of Gideon's writ of cert petition.

GIDeon's compLaInT

Exactly what was Gideon's complaint in his writ of certiorari? It stemmed from the following exchange between himself and the trial judge. Gideon had just asked the judge to appoint a defense lawyer for him. The words are taken directly from the transcript, or written record, of Gideon's trial.

> THE COURT [Judge Robert L. McCrary, Jr.]: Mr. Gideon, I am sorry, but I cannot appoint counsel to represent you in this case. Under the laws of the State of Florida, the only time the court can appoint counsel to represent a Defendant is when that person is charged with a capital offense [an offense punishable by death]. I am sorry, but I will have to deny your request to appoint counsel to defend you in this case.

> THE DEFENDANT [Gideon]: The United States Supreme Court says I am entitled to be represented by Counsel.

In his writ of cert, Gideon stated that "I was made to stand trial without the aid of counsel, and, at all times of my incarseration. The said Court refused to appoint counsel and therefore deprived me of due process of law; and violated my rights in the Bill of Rights and the constitution of the United States."

Though he was not a highly educated man, Gideon knew a few things about the law. While serving his prison sentence, he had used his time to learn about the U.S. Constitution. Gideon knew that the Sixth Amendment to

FeDeraL crimes versus sTaTe crimes

Federal courts handle most cases in which federal authorities, such as FBI agents or federal marshals, arrest the
suspect for a federal crime. This includes smuggling or
selling large amounts of narcotics, bank robbery, and
crimes committed on federal land.

State courts handle most cases in which the suspect
was arrested by a local police force. Typical state crimes
include burglary, assault and battery, rape, and murder.

the Constitution entitled defendants to a lawyer. He also
knew that Section 1 of the Fourteenth Amendment contains these words: "No state shall . . . deprive any person
of life, liberty, or property, without due process of law; nor
deny to any person within its jurisdiction the equal protection of the laws."

This sentence contains what are called the due-
process and the equal-protection clauses of the
Fourteenth Amendment. Together, they guarantee that
each person shall have his or her "day in court." In
Gideon's eyes, when the Florida trial court denied him a
defense lawyer, they denied him his day in court.

NeXT sTePS

After Gideon's writ was typed and printed, one of the
Court's law clerks summarized its contents, and then a
copy of the summary was sent to each of the nine justices.
Meanwhile, a printed copy of the cert was sent to Florida's
attorney general for a response. What did Florida's law
enforcement officials think of Gideon's claim that his
conviction in the state court should be reversed?

Because Gideon had filed the cert petition, he would be labeled the petitioner, while the director of Florida's prison system would be known as the respondent. On April 9, 1962, the Court received a reply from the respondent in the form of a brief, a document stating the facts and points of law in a case as the author sees them. According to the state of Florida, the state court had not denied Gideon his constitutional rights by refusing his request for a lawyer. As support, the respondent's brief quoted from a 1951 U.S. Supreme Court ruling in the case of *Gallegos* v. *Nebraska*: "The Federal Constitution does not command a state to furnish defendants counsel as a matter of course, as is required by the Sixth Amendment in federal prosecutions."

Like Gideon, the indigent defendant in *Gallegos* was prosecuted in a state court. If their cases had gone to federal courts instead, both Gideon and Gallegos would have been protected by this passage from the Sixth Amendment to the U.S. Constitution: "In all criminal prosecutions, the accused shall . . . have the assistance of counsel for his defense."

But it was understood that the Sixth Amendment applied only to federal courts. A state court *could* appoint a defense lawyer for an indigent defendant in a criminal trial, but it did not *have* to. Each state had its own laws in this regard. In Florida it was up to the trial judge. He would appoint a defense lawyer if he felt that the defendant was not capable of defending himself due to special circumstances, such as youth, ignorance of the law, illiteracy, or mental illness. The response from the state of Florida stated: "None of these exceptional circumstances were alleged [claimed] by petitioner [Gideon], and for that reason his petition for writ of certiorari should be denied."

Gideon was sent a copy of the Florida response. On

April 21, 1962, the U.S. Supreme Court received Gideon's response to the Florida response. Like his cert, it was handwritten in pencil. In this part of the response, he focuses on the issue of special circumstances: "It makes no difference how old I am or what color I am or what church I belong too if any. The question is I did not get a fair trial. The question is very simple. I requested the court to appoint me attorney and the court refused. . . ."

The nine justices now had copies of the following documents to consider:

> • Gideon's petition for certiorari to the U.S. Supreme Court
> • Gideon's earlier petition for writ of habeas corpus to the Florida State Supreme Court
> • The Florida State Supreme Court's denial of Gideon's petition for habeas corpus
> • The State of Florida's response to Gideon's petition for cert
> • Gideon's response to the State of Florida's response

Now it was up to the justices to decide whether to accept the case.

A SELECTIVE COURT

U.S. democracy is a complex form of government, and the U.S. Constitution is a complex document. In order to keep any one person or group from holding too much power, the framers of the Constitution designed an intricate system of dual governments, both state and federal. The judicial system reflects this duality, with courts at both federal and state levels.

At the top of the system sits the U.S. Supreme Court, the highest court in the land. Nearly all court cases, big

U.S. supreme court profile

The Supreme Court is the highest court in the United States. Among its defining characteristics are:

- The Supreme Court is created by Article III, Sections 1 and 2, of the U.S. Constitution.
- The Court meets regularly in the Supreme Court Building located at 1 First Street, Washington, D.C.
- It has nine members, known as justices. One is the chief justice, and the other eight are associate justices. The justices are appointed for life by the president, with the advice and consent of the Senate, and can be removed only by resignation or impeachment.
- The Supreme Court is charged with ensuring that all citizens receive equal justice under the law and that the rights guaranteed them by the Constitution are protected.
- Juries are not involved in Supreme Court cases. Instead, the Court reviews lower court decisions that raise conflicts between the Constitution and federal or state law. Its rulings are meant to preserve the Constitution.
- Once the Court makes a ruling, the other U.S. courts are expected to follow its decisions in similar cases.

and small, are decided in a lower court or courts at the state or federal levels. Only a tiny percentage of cases are ever appealed, by cert, to the nation's highest court. And the Court can accept only a small percentage of those certs for review. In 1962, over 2,500 certs were filed, but only 150 were selected.

What are the justices looking for when they decide which certs to select? First, the petition must focus on questions of federal, not state, law. It must deal with questions of constitutional law that apply to all the states. Gideon's case met this guideline, since it focused on two U.S. constitutional amendments, the Sixth and the Fourteenth.

Second, these questions must be important ones. Supreme Court Rule 10 states, "Review of a writ of certiorari is not a matter of right, but of judicial discretion. A petition for a writ of certiorari will be granted only for compelling reasons."

The Court was not primarily concerned with whether Gideon himself had received a fair trial. The justices were chiefly concerned with these constitutional issues: Could we say that an indigent defendant who was denied a lawyer and then convicted in a state criminal court received a fair trial? Could this defendant's trial be called "due process of law"? Or did lack of a defense attorney mean that he had been denied "equal protection of the laws"?

THE RIGHT TIME

The U.S. Supreme Court's powers are limited. The Court can't do what the president and members of Congress can do. It can't propose and pass new laws to help solve society's problems. But the Court can—and does—stay on the alert for problems that new laws could help solve. Then it looks for certs that address these issues.

At another time in history, the Court might have

passed over Gideon's cert. It might not have caught the justices' attention. But the cert arrived at the right time. The Court was on the lookout for appeals that dealt with an indigent defendant's right to a lawyer in state trials. That's why, on June 4, 1962, the Court announced that Clarence Earl Gideon's petition for cert had been granted.

TWO
GIDEON GETS A LAWYER

SUPREME COURT APPEALS are argued by lawyers for the two sides, petitioner and respondent. This time Gideon would have a lawyer to argue his case. The Supreme Court appoints a lawyer, free of charge, for any indigent prisoner whose appeal they accept. On June 22, 1962, the justices held a conference to decide on who that lawyer would be.

Whoever they chose for Gideon, he or she would receive a very small amount of money. The Court would pay the lawyer's transportation costs between home and Washington, D.C., and the printing costs for the brief the lawyer would have to prepare and present to the court.

But that would be all. There would be no money for the many hours that would go into preparing the brief and making the argument before the nine justices. On the other hand, arguing a case before the U.S. Supreme Court would be a huge honor and could mean a big boost to a lawyer's career.

The justices decided to appoint Abe Fortas, a partner in Arnold, Fortas, & Porter, one of Washington, D.C.'s largest and most highly respected law firms. Gideon could not have wished for better counsel. Fortas not only had experience arguing cases before the Court, he also firmly believed in the principles that Gideon's case stood for.

BESIDES PRACTICING LAW, ABE FORTAS SERVED AS A JUSTICE ON THE U.S. SUPREME COURT.

Pro Bono

Lawyers whom the U.S. Supreme Court appoints to represent indigent prisoners like Gideon are not paid for their time. They do the work *pro bono*. This Latin phrase means "for the good." That is, for the good of the public.

Some U.S. law firms take on a few pro bono cases involving indigent people each year, representing them in state and federal courts. It's a tradition among these firms to give some of their time and resources to help indigent defendants with their trial cases and indigent prisoners with their appeals.

Other law firms do pro bono work for other social causes. Some help victims of natural disasters, such as hurricanes, earthquakes, and floods. Some give legal aid to victims of domestic violence. Others help poor communities develop more economic resources, such as affordable housing and jobs.

LOOKING AT THE JUDGE

One of Fortas's first moves was to get a transcript of Gideon's trial to see what he could learn. He was looking for signs that Gideon had not gotten his proper "day in court" as guaranteed by the Constitution.

The first sign was Judge McCrary's statement that "Under the laws of the State of Florida, the only time the court can appoint counsel to represent a Defendant is when that person is charged with a capital offense."

The judge was plainly wrong. While Florida state law did not order him to appoint a lawyer for Gideon free of charge, it did not forbid it either. Judge McCrary could have gotten Gideon a defense lawyer no matter what crime Gideon was charged with.

And did the judge take time to find out whether Gideon met any of the special circumstances that would normally entitle him to a lawyer? The trial transcript showed no evidence that Judge McCrary had made any attempt to evaluate Gideon's ability to defend himself.

SELECTING THE JURY

Did the way that Gideon handled his defense show that he had done a capable job? One of Gideon's first crucial tasks as his own defense attorney was to help select the jury. Naturally, a defense attorney wants jurors who will be sympathetic toward his client.

In Florida a jury for a criminal trial consisted of six people in all, selected by the prosecuting attorney and the defense attorney from a larger pool of potential jurors. The attorneys would question potential jurors to decide which ones were most likely to vote for their side.

But Gideon did not ask a single question of anyone in the jury pool. Instead, he simply accepted the six individuals, all men, that the prosecuting attorney had selected. It looked like Gideon had no idea what the jury selection process was all about. Fortas also noted that the judge never informed Gideon that he could question potential jurors and reject those who seemed biased for the prosecution and against the defense.

QUESTIONING WITNESSES

A criminal trial begins with the prosecution presenting its case against the defendant. The most important witness testifying for the prosecution was Henry Cook of Panama City, Florida. Cook testified that he was there on the morning of June 3, 1961, outside the poolroom, and that he saw Gideon, whom he knew by sight, at the scene of the crime.

At 5:30 AM, Cook said, he spotted Gideon inside the

voir dire: FINDING THE RIGHT jury

When attorneys question potential jurors, the process is known as *voir dire*. Individually, these French words mean "to see" and "to hear." Together, they mean "to speak the truth."

During voir dire, the opposing attorneys present potential jurors with a series of questions in hopes that their answers will reveal who among them would be likely to vote for their side and who would not. First, potential jurors fill out a questionnaire. Then the attorneys ask them face-to-face questions. Each attorney may reject a certain number of potential jurors who seem biased against their side.

Experienced attorneys take time to carefully craft each voir dire question. If Gideon had had a good lawyer, that lawyer would have asked questions such as the following. As you read them, imagine that you are Gideon's lawyer, and think about the kinds of answers that would make you want to select or reject that person as a juror.

Have you or anyone in your family ever been the victim of a burglary?

What do you think about criminal defense lawyers?

How would you feel if you were falsely accused of doing something you did not do?

Do you believe that there ought to be rules so that anyone in this country can get a fair trial?

Do you think that someone who is accused of a crime is probably guilty of that crime?

building. Then he saw Gideon walk out of the poolroom with a bottle of wine and make a call on the pay phone at the corner. A few minutes later, a cab that Gideon apparently had called came and picked him up. After that, Cook said, he went into the poolroom, saw the damage, and realized that Gideon had broken in and robbed the place.

Then it was the defense's turn to cross-examine Cook. Instead of a defense counsel, Gideon himself would be asking the questions. Cook had just given eyewitness testimony that was extremely damaging to Gideon's case. Cook himself was a convicted felon. He had stolen a car. Gideon asked him about his criminal record, but Cook lied and said he had none, and Gideon let it go at that.

Either Gideon did not feel that Cook's criminal record was important for the jury to know about, or he didn't know that Cook was a convicted felon. A good defense lawyer would have known—and would have made sure that the jury found out about it during Cook's cross-examination. But Gideon asked Cook only a few more harmless questions, and the jury never learned of Cook's criminal record.

THE CASE FOR THE DEFENSE

Not once during the prosecution's case had Gideon made a single objection. Then it was Gideon's turn to present the case for the defense. Acting as his own lawyer, he called six witnesses in all. The first two were Bay Harbor's deputy sheriff and the police officer who discovered the break-in. A competent defense attorney never would have called law enforcement officers to the stand on his client's behalf unless they had helpful testimony to offer. Nothing the deputy or the officer had to say helped Gideon's case in the least.

The next witness for the defense was Preston Bray, the cab driver who picked him up that morning near the crime scene. Bray testified that he knew that Gideon sometimes worked there. A good lawyer would have asked more questions about Gideon's job at the poolroom. It gave Gideon a legitimate reason for being there that morning. But Gideon let this golden opportunity slip away.

Bray also said that Gideon might have been drunk that morning. Gideon asked Bray more questions on this subject until Bray changed his testimony and admitted that Gideon probably was not drunk after all. Here, Gideon was trying to protect his reputation. He did not want the jury to think of him as a drunk. But a good lawyer would have done the opposite. Under Florida law, being drunk could be used as a defense against a crime such as burglary. Gideon did not realize that he was actually working against himself.

The remaining three defense witnesses did Gideon's cause no more good than the first three. The case presented for the defense was of little help to the defendant.

THe sentence

After reading the transcript, two things were quite clear to Fortas: Gideon was not capable of defending himself in a court of law, and with a good defense attorney the result would almost certainly have been different. One of Fortas's associates at Arnold, Fortas, & Porter put it this way: "A lawyer—not a great lawyer, just an ordinary, competent lawyer—could have made ashes of the case."

Gideon's lack of legal skills carried over into the sentencing phase of the trial. The maximum punishment for the crime Gideon was charged with—the felony charge of breaking and entering along with the intent to commit a misdemeanor—was five years in prison. And that is just what Judge McCrary gave him: the maximum.

Before McCrary passed sentence, Gideon could have made a statement telling why he thought he should get a lighter sentence. A good defense lawyer would have done just that, and it might have helped. It certainly couldn't have hurt Gideon's cause. But Gideon made no statement to help himself.

After examining the trial transcript, Fortas saw that a number of mistakes had been committed that supported Gideon's petition of cert. The judge had made some of them. One was in leaving Gideon to defend himself. Gideon himself had made the rest of the mistakes. And his errors showed that he was not really capable of defending himself in a court of law.

GIDEON'S CHARACTER

Highlighting the mistakes made in the trial would be one key to winning the case. Another key would be Gideon himself. Who was this man? What sort of life had he led?

Fortas asked Gideon to write him a letter telling Fortas about himself. From his cell in the Florida State Prison, Gideon composed a document that gave Fortas an in-depth look at the character of the man he was defending.

Clarence Earl Gideon was born in 1910. That made him fifty-two years old. During his life he had served four different prison terms for burglary. None of the crimes involved any violence.

"I suppose, I am what is called individualist a person who will not conform," Gideon wrote. "Anyway my parents were always quarreling and I would be the scapegoat of those quarrels. My life was miserable. I was never allow to do the things of a ordinory boy. At the age of fourteen year, I ran away from home, I accepted the life of a hobo and tramp in preference to my home."

So, we see that the youthful Clarence Earl Gideon was a willful person and a loner determined not to lead the kind of life that the people around him led. Instead, he cut loose from ordinary life and took off on the road.

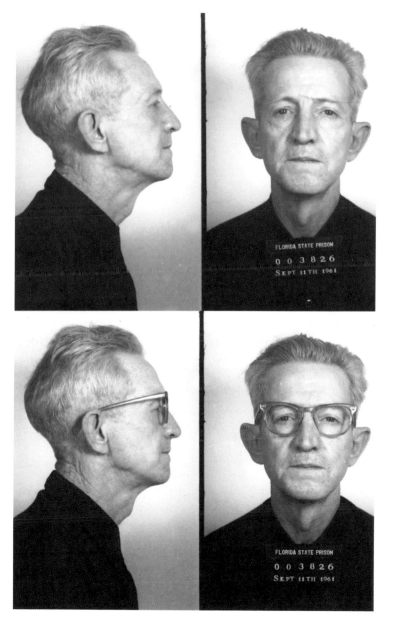

POLICE PHOTOS OF CONVICTED CRIMINALS ARE KNOWN AS MUG SHOTS. THESE ARE MUG SHOTS OF CLARENCE EARL GIDEON WITH AND WITHOUT HIS GLASSES.

But it was not the romantic, adventurous life of the carefree nonconformist that Gideon found. Instead, it was the hard life of a perpetual drifter and petty thief. Instead of freedom, he kept finding himself behind prison walls. First, at age fourteen, it was a stretch in a reformatory. Then it was in and out of different prisons, escaping from some, serving out his sentence in others.

Between prison times, Gideon did lots of gambling. But he also made attempts to rejoin ordinary society and lead a normal life. He held several legitimate jobs. He worked in a shoe factory. He was a railroad brakeman and cook. He also got married and had children.

But Gideon couldn't handle the responsibilities that came with family life. The State took his children away and put them in foster homes. Periods of bad health contributed to his problems, and so did getting hooked on drugs.

At this point, Gideon wrote to Fortas, he still hoped to get his children back and care for them. "I do not intend to let anyone take my children away from me and I will fight it every way I know how."

Here is how Gideon ended his letter:

I am not proud of this biography. I hope that it may help you in preparing this case, I am sorry I could not write better I have done the best I could. . . . Thank you for reading all of this. Please try to believe that all I want now from life is the chance for the love of my children the only real love I have ever had.

Gideon's determination to regain custody of his children from the State echoed the determination he expressed in his cert to regain his freedom, also taken by the State. Here was a man who, despite all his personal problems and failings, had not given up hope.

Three
A Look at the Past

NOW THAT FORTAS KNEW THE BASICS about the case and his client, how was he going to convince the nine justices that Gideon was right about being denied his constitutional rights? Fortas knew that the case would rest largely on the Sixth Amendment to the Constitution, which spoke of a person's right to an attorney in criminal cases. How did this amendment come about?

Common Law
The Sixth Amendment is rooted in English common law. Common laws are different from written laws. They are principles of law based on tradition. Even though common laws are not written down, courts still follow them.

The common law of England, before the nineteenth century, did not allow a person accused of a serious crime to be effectively represented by counsel. It didn't matter whether the accused was rich or poor. A lawyer could argue certain legal points suggested by the accused, but this lawyer could not present a real case on the defendant's behalf.

This denial of effective counsel was part of a general attitude of disrespect toward criminal defendants. People accused of crimes could not even see the charges against them before their trial. During the trial, they were not allowed to testify or to call witnesses on their own behalf.

The colonists who came to North America from England were experienced in England's common law. Many of them were also determined to avoid certain parts of it—including the part that so harshly limited the rights of the accused in courts of law. So the Founding Fathers had this right to counsel written into the Constitution as part of the Bill of Rights: the Sixth Amendment. Actually, all ten amendments in the Bill of Rights, ratified in 1791, were aimed at limiting the federal government's power over state governments and individual citizens. Outspoken critics such as Thomas Jefferson lobbied heavily for the Bill of Rights. These critics argued that without the amendments' restraints, the central government might resort to the same tyrannical tactics used by the British government and its kings and queens.

THE FOURTEENTH AMENDMENT

By 1962, it was understood that the Sixth Amendment protected all defendants in federal criminal trials. But in state courts, only defendants accused of capital crimes had to be given a court-appointed attorney. A capital crime is one that is punishable by a sentence of death. The big constitutional question facing Fortas was this: Could the Court be persuaded to widen the Sixth Amendment right to counsel and make it apply to all defendants in state criminal trials?

It is commonly understood that the Founding Fathers intended the Bill of Rights as a series of protections against a potentially tyrannical federal government only. They did not intend these protections to limit the power of state governments too.

But that understanding had been slowly but surely changing, step by step. The first step came in 1868, when the Fourteenth Amendment was ratified. The part of the amendment known as the due-process clause required

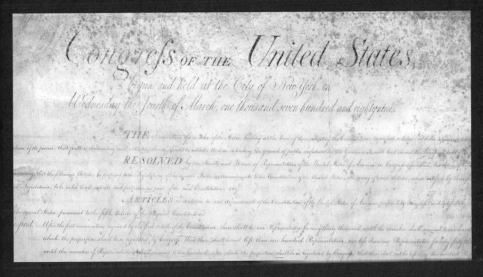

THE SIXTH AMENDMENT

In all criminal prosecutions, the accused shall enjoy the right to a speedy and public trial, by an impartial jury of the state and district wherein the crime shall have been committed, which district shall have been previously ascertained by law, and to be informed of the nature and cause of the accusation; to be confronted with the witnesses against him; to have compulsory process for obtaining witnesses in his favor, and to have the assistance of counsel for his defense.

states to extend some protections in the Bill of Rights to all people in their jurisdictions: "No State shall make or enforce any law which shall . . . deprive any person of life, liberty, or property, without due process of law."

But which protections would be extended to the states? The due-process clause did not say. It would be up to the U.S. Supreme Court to ultimately decide which rights from the Bill of Rights were covered by the phrase "life, liberty, or property."

In 1962, when Fortas began building his case for Gideon, this much was certain: The First Amendment freedoms of speech, press, and religion were covered; the states could not deprive people of these freedoms. The same could be said of the Fourth Amendment protection against unreasonable searches and seizures and the Eighth Amendment's prohibition against cruel and unusual punishments.

But the Court still saw Sixth Amendment protections as limited. They did apply to all defendants in federal criminal cases, but in state criminal cases they were seen applying only to defendants accused of capital crimes. Gideon had been tried in a state—not a federal—court, and his crime was a felony, not a capital crime.

How could Fortas get the Court to extend this Sixth Amendment protection to defendants like Gideon? The Court had been wrestling with this issue for decades. Fortas would have to reach back into the past to show the Court how its past decisions pointed in the direction of extending this protection.

POWELL V. ALABama

The Court's past decisions are known as precedent. The Court often uses precedent to help decide a later case involving a similar question of law. Fortas knew that the justices would expect both sides to refer to certain

Magna Carta

In his *Griffin* opinion, Justice Hugo L. Black refers back some 750 years to the legal document that laid the groundwork for equal justice for poor and rich alike: the Magna Carta. The year was 1215, the place was England, and the situation was dire indeed. English monarchs enjoyed absolute rule, and the current English king, John, was the most powerful in all of Europe. He could,

THE MAGNA CARTA WAS ORIGINALLY WRITTEN IN LATIN AND LATER TRANSLATED INTO ENGLISH.

and did, order the arrest and imprisonment of his enemies without any kind of trial. And he kept demanding more and more tax money from his subjects, who grew to hate him more and more.

The Magna Carta, Latin for "Great Charter," changed all that. The Barons, English noblemen, banded together to revolt against John's absolute power. They and their men took London by storm and occupied the city until King John agreed to sign the Magna Carta. Now English monarchs had to accept the fact that their power was no longer absolute, that the will of the king could be bound by law.

Historians and judicial scholars consider the Magna Carta to be the first in a long series of steps leading to the rule of constitutional law. From then on, the charter states, "No freemen shall be taken or imprisoned . . . except by the lawful judgment of his peers or by the law of the land."

important cases dealing with a defendant's right to an attorney in a criminal trial.

Powell v. *Alabama* (1932) was one of these landmark cases. At that point in legal history, federal courts had to appoint attorneys for any defendant who could not afford to hire one. But state courts did not have to appoint lawyers for indigent defendants no matter what crime they were charged with. *Powell* changed that situation.

The defendants in *Powell* became known as the Scottsboro Boys, for the town in rural Alabama where they were held after their arrest. There were nine of them, and they were all young, uneducated, and indigent. They were also African American, and they were accused of raping two white women. Rape was a capital crime, with the possible punishment of death.

TRIED AND CONVICTED

The Alabama state court that tried the defendants appointed two attorneys for them. One, Stephen Roddy, was a real estate lawyer. The other, Milo Moody, was known for his forgetfulness and had not tried a court case in decades. By no stretch of the imagination was either one an experienced criminal lawyer. Clearly, the state court was not doing the nine defendants any favor by appointing Roddy and Moody as their counsel.

Still, it looked as though the Scottsboro Boys might not be convicted. The prosecution's case was a weak and unconvincing one. The only evidence against the nine young men came from the testimony of the two girls who claimed they'd been raped. But the doctor who examined the girls, two hours after the alleged assaults had taken place, found no signs that they had been raped, beaten, and bloodied, as they claimed.

But in separate trials that each took only a day to complete, all but one of the nine were convicted and sentenced to death. On appeal, the Alabama State Supreme Court let stand all but one of these convictions. This left seven of the original nine Scottsboro Boys still behind bars.

THE RULING

Later, their convictions were appealed to the U.S. Supreme Court, and the Court found in their favor, reversing their convictions. The key to the Court's ruling lay in this passage:

> [I]n a capital case, where the defendant is unable to employ counsel, and is incapable adequately of making his own defense because of ignorance, feeble-mindedness, illiteracy, or the like, it is the duty of the court, whether requested or not, to assign counsel for him as a necessary requisite of due process of law.

The ruling, by Justice George Sutherland, mentioned "the failure of the trial court to make an effective appointment of counsel." The Court saw Roddy's and Moody's defense as sorely lacking in both skill and enthusiasm. Justice Sutherland pointed out how difficult it was for a layman to defend himself in a court of law:

> Even the intelligent and educated layman has small and sometimes no skill in the science of law. If charged with crime, he is incapable, generally, of determining for himself whether the indictment is good or bad. He is unfamiliar with the rules of evidence. Left without the aid of counsel he may be put on trial without a proper charge, and convicted upon incompetent evidence, or evidence irrelevant to the issue or otherwise inadmissible. He lacks both the skill and knowledge

adequately to prepare his defense, even though he have a perfect one.

What, then, should be done? The ruling went on to say:

He requires the guiding hand of counsel at every step in the proceedings against him. Without it, though he be not guilty, he faces the danger of conviction because he does not know how to establish his innocence. If that be true of men of intelligence, how much more true is it of the ignorant and illiterate, or those of feeble intellect.

Justice Sutherland stated that it would be a denial of due process of law for a court to deny a defendant the right to be represented by counsel. And the facts of this case, the ruling declared, amounted to a denial of "reasonable time and opportunity to secure counsel. . . . [T]he necessity of counsel was so vital and imperative that the failure of the trial court to make an effective appointment of counsel was likewise a denial of due process within the meaning of the Fourteenth Amendment."

A LanDmarK WITH LImITS

Powell was a landmark case for two historic reasons. It marked the first time the U.S. Supreme Court had reversed a state criminal conviction because the defendant was denied his constitutional rights. And it marked the first time the Court had ruled that the U.S. Constitution entitled an indigent defendant to a court-appointed lawyer.

But the ruling that widened the Sixth Amendment right to counsel came with an important limitation attached. Here, Justice Sutherland states that limitation:

Whether this would be so in other criminal prosecutions, or under other circumstances, we need
not determine. All that it is necessary now to
decide . . . is that in a capital case, where the defendant is unable to employ counsel . . . it is the duty of
the court, whether requested or not, to assign
counsel for him as a necessary requisite of due
process of law.

Those words "in a capital case" meant that a defendant
like Gideon would not benefit from this decision, since
Gideon was not tried for a capital crime. If a state trial
judge, such as Judge McCrary, chose not to appoint him an
attorney, Gideon still would have to defend himself.

So, to summarize: Before *Powell*, state courts did not
have to appoint lawyers for indigent defendants in criminal trials. After *Powell*, state courts had to appoint lawyers
for indigent defendants, but only for those accused of
capital crimes.

EQUAL JUSTICE

The limitations in the *Powell* ruling showed that the U.S.
Supreme Court was still reluctant to interfere in the judicial business of the states. Not that the Court could not
interfere in state judicial affairs. It could and did. A landmark case from 1816, *Martin* v. *Hunter's Lesee*, established
that the Court had both the power and the duty to help
establish uniformity in state court decisions.

This concept of uniformity goes back to the democratic
ideal that all people have the constitutional right to be
treated justly and equally. Above the main west entrance to
the U.S. Supreme Court building these words are carved in
stone: "Equal Justice Under Law." When some states deny
certain people equal justice, the Court may step in and set
down uniform standards of law for all the states.

The Court ruling in *Brown* v. *Board of Education* (1954) is a well-known example of the Court using its power to establish uniformity of law. In 1954, some states still had laws that forced black children to attend schools separate from white children. These laws were part of the "separate but equal" doctrine, laid down in the 1896 U.S. Supreme Court ruling known as *Plessy* v. *Ferguson*.

The *Brown* ruling stated that black children in the states of Kansas, South Carolina, Virginia, and Delaware "had been denied admission to schools attended by white children under laws requiring or permitting segregation according to race. This segregation was alleged to deprive the plaintiffs of the equal protection of the laws under the Fourteenth Amendment."

In its 1954 *Brown* ruling, the Court overturned *Plessy* and declared those state segregation laws unconstitutional. From then on, the laws in regard to school segregation were uniform: it was illegal in all fifty states. Now Fortas, acting on Gideon's behalf, was planning to ask the Court to make state laws uniform in regard to appointing a defense attorney for an indigent defendant.

JOHNSON V. ZERBST

The Court took another step toward strengthening the Sixth Amendment right to an attorney with its ruling in *Johnson* v. *Zerbst* (1938). *Johnson* took *Powell* a step further. Johnson and codefendant Bridwell (no first names were given in court documents) were accused of a federal crime: passing counterfeit money. The defendants, both U.S. Marines, were indigent. But their request for an attorney was denied because they were not accused of a capital crime. Johnson and Bridwell were tried in a federal court in South Carolina and convicted. Their sentence: four and a half years in a federal prison.

EVEN AFTER THE SUPREME COURT DECISION IN *BROWN* V. *BOARD OF EDUCATION*, MANY U.S. SCHOOLS REMAINED SEGREGATED. HERE, IN 1957, ARKANSAS NATIONAL GUARDSMEN KEEP AN AFRICAN-AMERICAN GIRL FROM ENTERING AN ALL-WHITE HIGH SCHOOL IN LITTLE ROCK.

During the trial, defendant Bridwell tried his best to defend himself: "I objected to one witness' testimony. I didn't ask him any questions, I only objected to his whole testimony. After the prosecuting attorney was finished with the witness, he said, 'Your witness,' and I got up and objected to the testimony on the grounds that it was all false, and the Trial Judge said any objection I had I would have to bring proof or disproof."

Like Gideon, Bridwell objected to testimony he claimed he knew to be false. And, like Gideon, Bridwell did not know how to question the witness to help prove this. In the ruling on *Johnson* v. *Zerbst*, Justice Hugo Black wrote:

> The average defendant does not have the professional legal skill to protect himself when brought before a tribunal with power to take his life or liberty, wherein the prosecution is presented by experienced and learned counsel. That which is simple, orderly, and necessary to the lawyer to the untrained layman may appear intricate, complex, and mysterious.

MORE LIMITATIONS

Black went on to explain how the *Johnson* ruling changed the way courts would interpret the Sixth Amendment. The amendment now required that courts appoint counsel for indigent defendants in federal criminal cases involving any felony, not only a capital crime.

But like *Powell*, *Johnson* came with limitations. The Court stopped short of extending the same right to counsel to indigent defendants in state courts. *Johnson* left state courts to decide for themselves whether to extend the right to counsel to indigent defendants accused of noncapital crimes.

To summarize, before *Johnson*, federal courts only had to appoint lawyers for indigent defendants accused of a capital crime. After *Johnson*, federal courts had to appoint lawyers for indigent defendants accused of a felony or a capital crime. But *Johnson* did not change how the states treated indigent defendants in regard to their right to an attorney.

NEXT ON THE LIST of precedent-setting cases was
Betts v. *Brady* (1942). To say that *Betts* was an important
case would be putting it mildly. In granting Gideon's writ,
the Court had written: "In addition to other questions
presented by this case, counsel are requested to discuss
the following in their briefs and oral argument: 'Should
this Court's holding in *Betts* v. *Brady* be reconsidered?'"

The Court was saying that in order for Gideon to win,
Fortas would have to persuade the justices to overturn a
ruling that the Court had made twenty years before.

Betts had been a controversial ruling since June 1,
1942, the day it was announced. The decision brought an
abrupt halt to a trend that had begun ten years earlier with
the *Powell* ruling. Taken together, *Powell* and *Johnson*
strengthened the rights of indigent defendants in criminal cases. Then came the roadblock of *Betts*. As you read
the facts in *Betts*, notice the similarities to *Gideon*.

THE FACTS IN THE CASE

Betts, an out-of-work farmhand, was arrested in Carroll
County, Maryland, and charged with robbery. (Betts's
first name was never given in court records. This is also
true in many of the cases that follow.) Betts was indigent,
so he asked for a court-appointed lawyer. The judge said
he could only appoint counsel for indigent defendants

who were accused of murder or rape. That left Betts with no choice but to defend himself against the robbery charge. He did his best but was found guilty and sentenced to eight years behind bars.

From prison, Betts filed a writ of habeas corpus, saying that the judge's refusal to appoint him a lawyer violated his constitutional rights. But the Maryland State Court of Appeals disagreed and denied the writ.

So Betts's last chance for relief lay with the U.S. Supreme Court. The Court accepted Betts's petition of certiorari because of the *Powell* limitation. That limitation said that state courts must appoint lawyers for indigent defendants charged with a capital crime, but that "whether this would be so in other criminal prosecutions, or under other circumstances, we need not determine."

Now, ten years later, the Court decided that the time had come to make that determination: "The question we are now to decide is whether due process of law demands that in every criminal case, whatever the circumstances, a state must furnish counsel to an indigent defendant."

THE RULING

The justices ruled 6 to 3 against Betts. They based their decision largely on a review of individual state constitutions. How did the states handle the issue? The ruling explains what the justices found in their review:

> This material demonstrates that, in the great majority of the states, it has been the considered judgment of the people, their representatives, and their courts that appointment of counsel is not a fundamental right, essential to a fair trial. . . . In the light of this evidence, we are unable to say that the concept of due process incorporated in the Fourteenth Amendment obligates the

States, whatever may be their own views, to furnish counsel in every such case.

So, after *Betts*, state courts still did not have to
appoint counsel for indigent defendants accused of a
non-capital crime under normal circumstances. But
state courts would have to appoint counsel in the event of
what the Court called special circumstances amounting to
"a denial of fundamental fairness, shocking to the uni-
versal sense of justice."

These special circumstances included the defendant's
inability to read or write, his youth, a mental illness, or
improper conduct on the part of the prosecutor or judge.
But these examples were only suggestions. The Court
warned against "the danger of falling into the habit of for-
mulating the guarantee into a set of hard and fast rules."
Instead, state courts were supposed to use "the totality of
facts in a given case," including special circumstances, to
determine whether a defendant was incapable of
defending himself.

A DoubLe STanDarD

With the *Betts* ruling, the Court declared that in state
criminal trials, a defendant need not be represented by a
lawyer to receive a fair trial, except in certain special circumstances. Yet with its earlier ruling in *Johnson* v. *Zerbst*
(1938), the Court had declared that in federal criminal
trials, all defendants, regardless of their circumstances,
must be represented by counsel. Thus, the Court approved
of one standard for federal courts and an opposite standard for state courts.

In the 6 to 3 *Betts* decision, Justice Hugo L. Black was
one of the three justices in the minority. He voted against
the majority ruling. Justices in the minority may write
their own dissenting opinions in a case, explaining why

they disagree with the majority. While their dissents are not law, they are published along with the majority ruling and may influence future Court decisions.

Black did not just disagree with the majority decision—he was passionately against it. In his dissent, Black wrote: "Whether a man is innocent cannot be determined from a trial in which, as here, denial of counsel has made it impossible to conclude, with any satisfactory degree of certainty, that the defendant's case was adequately presented."

Black went on to point out the need to "assure that no man shall be deprived of counsel merely because of his poverty. Any other practice seems to me to defeat the promise of our democratic society to provide equal justice under the law."

FIVE
BEYOND *BETTS*

IN THE years after *BETTS*, every right-to-counsel case in a state criminal court was subject to *Betts*'s "special circumstances" and "totality of facts" standards. But what were these standards exactly? The Court had stopped short of clearly defining and rating them in terms of importance. So it was up to individual state courts and judges to create their own sets of definitions and rating systems.

How well did this process work? The next two cases give us an idea.

uveges v. *pennsylvania* (1948)

Uveges (first name not given), a youth of seventeen, was charged with four burglaries. He pleaded guilty and received a sentence of twenty to forty years in a Pennsylvania prison. That was in 1938.

Eight years later, in 1946, Uveges sent a writ of habeas corpus to the Pennsylvania state court that sentenced him. The writ alleged that during the time between his arrest and sentencing, the court never told him that he had the right to a lawyer. Therefore, the court had deprived him of his constitutional right to counsel.

Uveges's writ was denied, so he turned to the U.S. Supreme Court, which accepted his case. Here, in Justice Stanley Reed's 1948 majority opinion, we see how deeply

WHEN LAWYERS AND IMPRISONED CLIENTS CONSULT, IT CAN LOOK SOMETHING
LIKE THIS.

divided the justices were on the issue of when a criminal
defendant should have a court-appointed lawyer:

> Some members of the Court think that where
> serious offenses are charged, failure of a court to
> offer counsel in state criminal trials deprives an
> accused of rights under the Fourteenth
> Amendment. . . . Others of us think that when a
> crime subject to capital punishment is not
> involved, each case depends on its own facts. See
> *Betts* v. *Brady*.

The *Uveges* opinion then looks closely at the issue of special circumstances from *Betts* and concludes: "Where the gravity of the crime and other factors [special circumstances]. . . render criminal proceedings without counsel so apt to result in injustice as to be fundamentally unfair . . . the accused must have legal assistance."

The Supreme Court found that the lower court did not take into account Uveges's youth and other special circumstances as ordered in *Betts* and should have appointed Uveges a defense attorney. So, by a 6 to 3 vote, the Court reversed Uveges's conviction due to special circumstances. What the Court was saying was that the state should have granted Uveges a lawyer but did not, ignoring the special circumstances involved.

McNeal v. *Culver* (1961)

In this case, a state court again fails to take into account special circumstances that show the indigent defendant's need for an attorney. Defendant McNeal was tried in a Florida court without counsel. He was convicted of assault to murder in the second degree and sentenced to twenty years in prison.

While serving his sentence, McNeal petitioned the U.S. Supreme Court. His petition of cert stated that he was indigent, ignorant, mentally ill, a Negro, and incapable of conducting his own defense. Therefore, by denying him an attorney despite special circumstances, the trial court had denied him due process of law.

> The need of counsel is the same, whatever the economic status of the accused. If due process requires that a rich man who wants a lawyer be allowed the opportunity to obtain one before he is tried, why should not due process give the same protection to the accused who is indigent?. . . *Betts*

v. *Brady* . . . is so at war with our concept of equal
justice under law that it should be overruled.

GRIFFIN V. ILLINOIS (1956)

This last landmark case does not deal with *Betts* and special circumstances. It focuses on another law affecting
indigent prisoners.

Under Illinois law a prisoner who wants to appeal
his criminal conviction must supply a written record of his
trial. Court transcripts cost money. If the prisoner could
not afford to pay, he was out of luck. He could not get a
transcript and so could not appeal his conviction. The
only exception was indigent prisoners sentenced to death.
Only they could get a free transcript.

This law was at the center of *Griffin* v. *Illinois*. Two
men, Griffin and Crenshaw, were tried together in the
Criminal Court of Cook County, Illinois, and convicted of
armed robbery. The men, both indigent, were kept from
appealing their case to an appellate court when they could
not pay for a transcript of their trial.

Eventually, Griffin and Crenshaw appealed to the U.S.
Supreme Court, which ruled 5 to 4 that the petitioners
were denied equal protection of laws guaranteed by the
Fourteenth Amendment. The Illinois law regarding transcripts was overturned. From then on, all fifty states had
to provide a free transcript to any indigent prisoner who
requested one.

In his majority opinion, Justice Black wrote about the
decision to make state laws uniform regarding transcripts:

Statistics show that a substantial proportion of
criminal convictions are reversed by state appellate courts. Thus to deny adequate review to the
poor means that many of them may lose their life,
liberty or property because of unjust convictions

THROUGH THE COURT SYSTEM

First Stop: State Court
Almost all cases (about 95 percent) start in state courts.
These courts go by various names, depending on the state
in which they operate: circuit, district, municipal, county,
or superior. The case is tried and decided by a judge, a
panel of judges, or a jury.
   The side that loses can then appeal to the next level.

First Stop: Federal Court
U.S. DISTRICT COURT—About 5 percent of cases begin
their journey in federal court. Most of these cases concern
federal laws, the U.S. Constitution, or disputes that
involve two or more states. They are heard in one of the
ninety-four U.S. district courts in the nation.
U.S. COURT OF INTERNATIONAL TRADE—Federal court
cases involving international trade appear in the U.S.
Court of International Trade.
U.S. CLAIMS COURT—The U.S. Claims Court hears federal cases that involve more than $10,000, Indian claims,
and some disputes with government contractors.
   The loser in federal court can appeal to the next level.

Appeals: State Cases
Forty states have appeals courts that hear cases that have
come from the state courts. In states without an appeals
court, the case goes directly to the state supreme court.

Appeals: Federal Cases
U.S. CIRCUIT COURT—Cases appealed from U.S. district
courts go to U.S. circuit courts of appeals. There are twelve
circuit courts that handle cases from throughout the

nation. Each district court and every state and territory are assigned to one of the twelve circuits. Appeals in a few state cases—those that deal with rights guaranteed by the U.S. Constitution—are also heard in this court.

U.S. COURT OF APPEALS—Cases appealed from the U.S. Court of International Trade and the U.S. Claims Court are heard by the U.S. Court of Appeals for the Federal Circuit. Among the cases heard in this court are those involving patents and minor claims against the federal government.

Further Appeals: State Supreme Court

Cases appealed from state appeals courts go to the highest courts in the state—usually called supreme court. In New York, the state's highest court is called the court of appeals. Most state cases do not go beyond this point.

Final Appeals: U.S. Supreme Court

The U.S. Supreme Court is the highest court in the country. Its decision on a case is the final word. The Court decides issues that can affect every person in the nation. It has decided cases on slavery, abortion, school segregation, and many other important issues.

The Court selects the cases it will hear—usually around one hundred each year. Four of the nine justices must vote to consider a case in order for it to be heard. Almost all cases have been appealed from the lower courts (either state or federal).

Most people seeking a decision from the Court submit a petition for certiorari. Certiorari means that the case will be moved from a lower court to a higher court for review. The Court receives about nine thousand of these requests annually. The petition outlines the case and gives reasons why the Court should review it.

In rare cases, for example *New York Times* v. *United States*, an issue must be decided immediately. When such a case is of national importance, the Court allows it to bypass the usual lower court system and hears the case directly.

To win a spot on the Court's docket, a case must fall within one of the following categories:

• Disputes between states and the federal government or between two or more states. The Court also reviews cases involving ambassadors, consuls, and foreign ministers.

• Appeals from state courts that have ruled on a federal question.

• Appeals from federal appeals courts (about two-thirds of all requests fall into this category).

which appellate courts would set aside. Many States have recognized this fact and provided aid for convicted defendants who have a right to appeal and need a transcript but are unable to pay for it. A few have not. Such a denial is a misfit in a country dedicated to affording equal justice to all and special privileges to none in the administration of its criminal law. There can be no equal justice where the kind of trial a man gets depends on the amount of money he has.

No official figures were available, but states estimated that 30 percent to 60 percent of all people convicted and sent to prison could not afford to hire a lawyer to defend them. These statistics show why the justices wanted to address the *Gideon* case.

SIX
THE BRIEFS

ABE FORTAS DID NOT prepare the case alone. He had expert help from his colleagues at Arnold, Fortas, & Porter. Together, they researched past cases, from *Powell* to *McNeal*, and engineered a point-by-point strategy to achieve their goal: persuading the Court to rule that not just Gideon but all people accused of a serious crime should be guaranteed a lawyer to defend them.

And that meant expanding the scope of the Fourteenth Amendment to include a defendant's right to a lawyer in a state criminal case. To do this expanding, the Court, an arm of the federal government, would have to impose its power on the states. It would have to force them all to abide by a single uniform law for appointing counsel.

Would the justices be willing to take this step? Past cases show that the Court was still deeply divided on the issue of how much power should rest with the central government and how much should remain in the hands of the states. How would Fortas achieve his goal? His next task was to outline the petitioner's case in the form of a brief. This was a written summary explaining how he would present his side when he and his opponent delivered their oral arguments before the justices. The brief is more than just a point-by-point preview of the oral argument, though. The petitioner's brief is the backbone of his case. So each point must be clear, complete, and above all, persuasive.

THe GreaT FeDeraLISm DeBaTe

How much power should rest with the federal government and how much with the individual states? The Constitution's framers designed a government where power is carefully divided between two coequal and interlocked political units: state and nation. *Federalism* is the word that describes this unique form of government.

The key to federalism lies in power-sharing. The Constitution outlines the "express powers" of the federal government, such as the right to raise taxes and declare war. It also gives the federal government the "implied power" to pass the laws that it needs in order to properly exercise those powers.

That leaves the "reserved powers" for the states. Those are the powers that the Constitution neither gives to the federal government nor forbids to the states. The Constitution's framers were wary of the federal government becoming tyrannical, as had happened in England. So the states were expected to exercise checks and balances on the national government to limit its power. This made for a dynamic ongoing power struggle between state and nation.

The Constitution sets out the grand plan of federalism. But it leaves open to debate exactly which powers belong to the states and which to the federal government. *Gideon* v. *Wainwright* is part of that ongoing debate.

PETITIONER'S POINT: DUE PROCESS

Question: Should the Fourteenth Amendment protection of due process apply to the Sixth Amendment right to an attorney for defendants accused of all serious crimes, not just capital crimes?

In his brief, Fortas wrote: "The due process clause protects against deprivation of 'liberty' and 'property' as well as against deprivation of 'life.'" That is, the Florida court unfairly imprisoned Gideon after denying him an attorney, thus depriving him of his liberty and denying him due process of law.

The brief also stated: "The indigent, apart from all other considerations, has probably been in jail from the time of arrest because of inability to furnish bail. How can he prepare his case?" That is, by depriving Gideon of his liberty between his arrest and trial, the state of Florida made it all but impossible for him to regain that liberty.

So, according to Fortas's argument, the due process clause of the Fourteenth Amendment demands that the courts appoint a defense lawyer in criminal cases for indigent defendants such as Gideon.

PETITIONER'S POINT: EQUAL PROTECTION

While preparing the brief, Fortas and his colleagues decided to focus on the equal protection clause of the Fourteenth Amendment as well as the due process clause.

From the brief: "Our accusatorial system of criminal justice presupposes that the cause of the defendant as well as that of the state will be vigorously advocated." That is, both sides in a criminal trial, not just one side, must have their "day in court." From the brief:

> In the case of those able financially to hire counsel,
> the rule is not limited to capital cases or to 'special
> circumstance.' It is absolute and complete, and a

state may not restrict it. . . . If this is so, counsel must be provided in all criminal cases in which there is a constitutional requirement to permit counsel to appear and act for those who have the funds to hire them. The indigent defendant cannot be denied an "unqualified right" solely because of poverty; to do so results in a denial of equal protection.

That is, if a person able to pay a lawyer has an absolute right to hire one, then denying that right to a person unable to pay violates the equal protection clause. It amounts to discrimination against the poor.

To strengthen his point Fortas cites precedent: "The principle was articulated in *Griffin* v. *Illinois* . . . which held that the Fourteenth Amendment requires that 'Destitute defendants must be afforded as adequate appellate review as defendants who have money enough to buy transcripts.'" So, Fortas's argument goes, if the Court says that a defendant who cannot pay for a transcript is entitled to one, then why is that defendant not also entitled to a lawyer?

PETITIONER'S POINT: HOW A LAWYER WOULD HAVE HELPED GIDEON

Fortas would need to show the justices how the trial would have been different if Gideon had been given counsel. And he would have to emphasize that this difference applied to all indigent defendants, not just Gideon. From the brief:

No individual who is not a trained or experienced lawyer can possibly know or pursue the technical, elaborate, and sophisticated measures which are necessary to assemble and appraise the facts, analyze the law, determine contentions, negotiate the pleas, or marshal and present all of the factual and legal considerations which have a bearing upon his defense.

The brief detailed some of the vital services a good defense lawyer can provide that a defendant such as Gideon cannot. A lawyer can decide whether the arrest was legal, whether the indictment is valid, whether a search and seizure of evidence was lawful, and whether a confession will be accepted in court as evidence. A lawyer can determine whether the defendant is really responsible for the crime he is charged with, or whether he should be charged with a lesser offense. A lawyer can know when to make objections to prosecution evidence and how to cross-examine witnesses.

From the transcript of Gideon's trial and trials of other indigent defendants forced to defend themselves, it was clear that these vital services were beyond the defendants' skills to provide. In short, the assistance of a lawyer was essential to a fair trial and so must be provided in the name of due process of law.

PeTITIONer's POINT: *BeTTS* V. *BraDY* BrINGS cONFUSION

To win the case, Fortas would have to get the Court to over-turn *Betts* v. *Brady*. So he and his team combed through the ruling, looking for anything that would support their cause.

Since the heart of *Betts* was the special circumstances provision, they made that provision their chief point of attack. To plan the attack, they examined all the rulings related to *Betts* that the Court had handed down since *Betts* was passed in 1942, including *Uveges* v. *Pennsylvania* and *McNeal* v. *Culver*.

The rulings mentioned ten different special circumstance factors. Among them were the defendant's age, education, mental ability, and skin color; the complexity of the law he was on trial for breaking; lack of help during the trial from the judge; and the prosecutor's misbehavior.

Such a long list was confusing. There was no way of knowing the relative importance of each circumstance. From the brief: "No standards have been delineated, however, with respect to the weight or importance to be assigned each of the foregoing factors."

So in each case each judge in each state had to take a new look at these special circumstances. He had to decide which of the long list of special circumstances applied to the defendant, if any, and whether the ones that did apply were serious enough to make a fair trial impossible without counsel.

Each judge's decision would depend greatly upon who was looking at the case and what this judge knew of the law. So the same case could qualify an indigent defendant for a court-appointed lawyer in one courtroom but not in another. Gideon's case was a prime example. Judge McCrary himself was confused about special circumstances. Another judge who knew the law in Florida better than McCrary might have granted Gideon's request.

PETITIONER'S POINT: OVERTURNING *BETTS* WOULD REDUCE CONFUSION

All these special circumstances led to a lot of guessing. In each case state courts had to guess when and how to apply these circumstances. And a wrong guess meant that the defendant, on appeal, could have the conviction reversed. Then the state would have to either set him free or try him all over again. From Fortas's brief: "[Special circumstances] is a rule which compels continual, unseemly, and improper intervention by the federal courts in state criminal proceedings—not on the basis of applying a concrete, fundamental principle but by the corrosive and irritating process of case-by-case review."

The brief compared these confusing consequences with the change that would be brought about if *Betts* were overturned and state courts had to appoint attorneys for indigent defendants. Making the law clear-cut and uniform in all fifty states would bring an end to all this confusion and guessing. It would also eliminate all the intervention by federal appeals courts, including the U.S. Supreme Court, in state criminal proceedings.

PETITIONER'S POINT: DEFENDANTS ARE BEING DENIED COUNSEL

In their study of past cases, Fortas and his team found that state courts seldom mention special circumstances to indigent defendants and that they nearly always reject defendants' requests for counsel. From the brief: "In the present case, the trial court did not call petitioner's attention to the 'special circumstances' bearing on the right to appointment of counsel. . . . [T]he 'special circumstances' rule has only infrequently led the state courts to appoint counsel."

What happened when indigent prisoners, claiming special circumstances, petitioned the Court to reverse their convictions because the state had denied them counsel? The Court had consistently ruled for the prisoner in these cases. In every single case the Court took up from 1950 to 1962, the justices had come to the same conclusion: By refusing to appoint counsel in a criminal trial, the state court had violated the defendant's constitutional rights in regard to due process of law.

PETITIONER'S POINT: MOST STATES ALREADY APPOINT COUNSEL

Fortas found that overturning *Betts* would not amount to anything like a judicial revolution. Why? Because this revolution had already taken place. In 1942, when *Betts* was passed, thirty states automatically provided counsel to indigent defendants. Now, in 1962, the number had grown to thirty-seven, and twenty-four of those states provided counsel not just for capital crimes and felonies, but for misdemeanor defendants as well.

That left only thirteen states that still did not have a statewide law assuring indigent defendants counsel. And eight of those thirteen states routinely appointed counsel in courts in their larger cities. Only Alabama, Florida, Mississippi, and North and South Carolina still did not make it a practice to appoint counsel for indigent defendants, except in capital cases. From the brief:

> There is no doubt that there is today widespread consensus among the states that legal assistance should be furnished to indigent persons. Further, it is a principle which has the overwhelming support of the bar [organizations of lawyers nationwide]. The task here is essentially a modest one: to bring into line with the consensus of the states and professional opinion the few "stragglers" who persist in denying fair treatment to the accused.

PETITIONER'S POINT: *BETTS* HAS NOT WORKED AS PLANNED

Fortas found that in nearly every case in which a defendant without a lawyer was convicted in a state court, the prisoner ended up appealing to federal courts to have his conviction reversed. From the brief: "The absence of counsel is responsible in large measure for the flood of habeas corpus petitions in the federal courts which create state-federal friction and constitute a burden on the federal system."

This flood of appeals made life difficult for state court judges, Fortas wrote. Their decisions were constantly being reviewed by federal judges and set aside. *Betts* was supposed to result in less interference by the federal government in state judicial affairs. Instead, it had brought more.

Requiring counsel in all state criminal prosecutions would help remedy this situation. Overturning *Betts* would actually give state courts relief from federal interference. Here, Fortas had a particularly persuasive point. It might win over the justices who were reluctant to impose the will of the federal government on the individual states by expanding the scope of the Fourteenth Amendment.

jacob versus Fortas

Fortas filed his *Gideon* brief with the Court on November 21, 1962. A copy also went to Gideon himself at the state prison in Raiford, Florida. As required, Fortas also mailed a copy to the Florida attorney general's office.

By tradition, a copy of the petitioner's brief goes to the respondent, who responds by writing a brief of his own. That task fell to Bruce Robert Jacob, assistant attorney general of the state of Florida, who would also argue the case before the justices. Jacob was twenty-six years old, exactly half Fortas's age, a young man with far less experience than his rival. Fortas already had argued cases before the U.S. Supreme Court; Jacob had never even set foot in the Court building before. But as later events would prove, Jacob knew a good deal about both law and politics.

Fortas's task was to persuade the justices to go against precedent and change the law. From Fortas's brief: *"Betts*

ASSISTANT ATTORNEY GENERAL BRUCE JACOB WAS ONLY TWENTY-SIX YEARS OLD WHEN HE ARGUED THE *GIDEON* CASE FOR THE STATE OF FLORIDA.

v. *Brady* should be overruled." Jacob's objective was to persuade the justices to stick with precedent and let *Betts* stand. From Jacob's brief: "*Betts* v. *Brady* should not be overruled or modified."

Which man had the more difficult job? As a general rule, justices are reluctant to go against precedent, since past cases give them a foundation on which to make new rulings. To be persuaded to strike down precedent-setting rulings such as *Betts*, they must have good, sound reasons. Some reasons to strike down precedent are based on the old saying: "Times change." That is, what worked in the past no longer works today because the ways in which we live our lives and look at the world have changed. Other reasons focus on the precedent-setting case itself: that something was fundamentally wrong with the ruling when it was passed and is still wrong today.

From reading Fortas's brief, Jacob knew that his opponent would claim that *Betts* was fundamentally wrong when it was passed. He also could see that Fortas had strong points in support of his claim. How could Jacob counter Fortas's points?

RESPONDENT'S POINT: DUE PROCESS

The justices would expect Jacob to address the same fundamental question as Fortas: Should the Fourteenth Amendment protection of due process be extended to include the right to an attorney for defendants accused of all serious crimes, not just capital crimes?

In his respondent's brief, Jacob wrote: "The Fourteenth Amendment does not constitute a 'shorthand summary' of the Bill of Rights; and the specific procedural guarantees of the . . . amendments are not included in the meaning of due process." And he wrote: "[A]utomatic appointment of counsel in all criminal cases has never been considered an essential of due process."

RESPONDENT'S POINT: THE SIXTH AMENDMENT RIGHT TO COUNSEL

So, according to Jacob, the Fourteenth Amendment due-process clause provides no basis for expanding the right to an attorney to include indigent defendants in state courts. But what about the Sixth Amendment right-to-counsel provision? From the respondent's brief:

> Historically, there is no basis for requiring the states to automatically appoint counsel in all cases. The English common law did not even provide a right to retain counsel, except in misdemeanor and

minor cases. The right to counsel provision of the Sixth Amendment, as of the time of its adoption . . . was not aimed to compel the states to provide counsel for a defendant.

And again, from the brief, Jacob addresses Gideon's case in particular: "The Sixth Amendment as originally intended guaranteed the right to retain counsel, not the right to have counsel appointed in cases of indigency."

Notice that Jacob writes of the Sixth Amendment "as originally intended." This is his way of emphasizing the respondent's point of view as to how the U.S. Constitution should be viewed: The document, including its amendments, should be interpreted strictly. We must be very careful about extending or expanding on any rights stated in the document itself. And since the Constitution makes no mention of the states providing counsel for indigent defendants, we cannot assume that it grants that right.

RESPONDENT'S POINT: THE TENTH AMENDMENT AND STATES' RIGHTS

Besides calling for a strict interpretation of the Constitution, Jacob's brief stands up for the right of state courts to be as free as possible from interference by federal courts, including the U.S. Supreme Court. From the brief: "Under the Tenth Amendment of the Constitution, all powers not granted to the central government were specifically reserved to the states. These reserved powers, including the power of the states to control proceedings in their own courts, cannot be diminished or modified."

Also from the respondent's brief: "A requirement that counsel be automatically appointed would infringe upon the historic right of the people of the states to determine their own rules of procedure and would defeat the very desirable possibility of experiment."

THe TenTH AmenDmenT

The powers not delegated to the United States by the Constitution, nor prohibited by it to the States, are reserved to the States respectively, or to the people.

That is, if the Court overruled *Betts* and made the law uniform, with all states automatically appointing counsel for indigent defendants, the power of the states would be diminished. Then individual states could no longer improve the criminal justice system by developing new strategies for deciding when to appoint legal counsel for indigent defendants.

RESPONDENT'S POINT: THe SPECIAL CIRCUMSTANCES PROVISION IS ADEQUATE

Fortas's complaints about the confusion with special circumstances could not be dismissed outright. But they could be countered.

Fortas called the special circumstances provision of *Betts* confusing. But, Jacob wrote, it provided a clear and consistent standard for determining right to counsel under the Fourteenth Amendment. In its rulings since *Betts* was passed, the Court itself had determined ten specific factors for the states to use as guidelines. Jacob listed them in the brief:

1. Gravity of the offense, i.e., whether capital or non capital. That is, the more serious the crime, the more a defendant needs counsel;
2. Complexity of the charge against the defendant. That is, the more complex the charge, the more

difficult it will be to understand, so the more likely that a defendant will need counsel;

3. Ignorance;

4. Illiteracy or lack of education;

5. Extreme youth or lack of experience;

6. Familiarity with court procedure. That is, repeat offenders are more familiar with trials than first-time offenders and so are less likely to need counsel;

7. Feeble-mindedness or insanity;

8. Inability to understand the English language;

9. Prejudicial conduct shown by trial judge, prosecuting attorney, or public defender;

10. Plea of guilty by co-defendant within hearing of jury.

While the special circumstances provision was not an ideal way to handle appointment of counsel, it was adequate. And it certainly was better than taking control away from the states by imposing upon them a single uniform code of criminal procedure. From the brief: "[D]ue process cannot be reduced to a mechanical formula in cases relating to any area of criminal procedure."

RESPONDENT'S POINT: GIDEON WAS COMPETENT TO DEFEND HIMSELF

In his defense of special circumstances, Jacob addressed Gideon's case in particular. From the brief:

> In his petition to the Florida Supreme Court, Gideon made no affirmative showing of any circumstances or unfairness which would have entitled him to counsel under the Fourteenth Amendment. He merely alleged that he was without funds and that he pleaded not guilty and

requested court appointed counsel while being
tried on a charge of breaking and entering with
intent to commit a misdemeanor.

That is, since Gideon made no claim of special circumstances, the court was under no obligation to grant
him an attorney. But was Clarence Earl Gideon, in fact,
entitled to special circumstances without knowing it?

No, Jacob said, he clearly was not. From the brief:
"Petitioner took an active role in his defense and showed
that he possessed much skill and facility in questioning
witnesses and handling himself in court."

To help prove his point, Jacob went over some of the
ten special circumstances listed on pages 68–69 as they
related to Gideon. Factor number six was familiarity with
court procedures. From the brief: "Petitioner's record
indicates that he 'was not wholly unfamiliar with criminal
procedure.'" Here, Jacob quotes from the *Betts* ruling,
saying that, like Betts, Gideon had been arrested, tried,
and imprisoned before. Therefore, Gideon already had
firsthand knowledge of how trial courts worked.

Gideon was also familiar with the charges against him
(factor number two). From the brief: "A charge of
breaking and entering with intent to commit petit larceny
is uncomplicated . . ."

RESPONDENT'S POINT: OVERTURNING *BETTS* WOULD BE COSTLY

To make this point, Jacob used the slippery slope argument. This argument is an assumption based on a well-
known fear about human behavior: that taking one step in
a direction we do not wish to go will inevitably lead to
another step in that same direction, and then another, on
and on down the slippery slope to disaster. From the brief:
"[To overturn *Betts*] would be to impose upon the states a

requirement to provide free counsel to defendants in all criminal cases, including misdemeanors."

While this might not happen right away, it could happen in time, according to the slippery slope way of thinking. And the result? Jacob's reasoning went something like this: Every day thousands of people appear in traffic court charged with misdemeanors, such as speeding, making an illegal turn, or parking illegally. What if every indigent person charged with any kind of crime, even a misdemeanor, could demand a court-appointed lawyer? How could the states possibly find the money to pay for all these lawyers? For that matter, how could there even be enough lawyers out there to handle all these cases, from capital crimes all the way down to the slightest misdemeanors?

If overturning *Betts* affected prisoners already in jail, it would be costly in another way, Jacob wrote. From the brief: "A decision reversing the present, if retroactive, will allow over 5,000 hardened criminals in Florida to be set free. Retrials of these prisoners will be impossible in many cases."

That is, overturning *Betts* might mean that every indigent prisoner convicted without counsel could file a habeas corpus petition that would lead to having his conviction reversed. The state courts were already clogged with cases. How could they find the time, money, and court-appointed defense attorneys to try these thousands of men again?

seven
AMICUS CURIAE

BOTH Bruce Jacob and Abe Fortas looked for support for their arguments. The lawyers welcomed help from people and organizations in the form of *amicus curiae* briefs.

Amicus curiae is Latin for "friend of the court." Individuals or groups who are especially interested in a case may file amicus curiae briefs on behalf of the petitioner or respondent. Justices receive copies to read and may be influenced by the arguments they present. Writers of these briefs may also be called upon to take part in the oral argument.

Jacob looked for help from other state officials. A state attorney general is the principal law officer in a state. Jacob naturally assumed that other state attorneys general would side with him to keep *Betts* in place for the same reasons he had expressed in his brief. So he mailed a letter to all forty-nine state attorneys general warning them that *Betts* could be overturned in the *Gideon* case, and asking them to write amicus curiae briefs supporting his side.

Attorneys general in Alabama and North Carolina responded. They both agreed that Gideon had done a good job of defending himself at his trial. They also stated that the average indigent defendant could do as good a job of defending himself as a professional defense attorney. Yes, they agreed, *Betts* should not be overturned.

support from Alabama

Assistant Attorney General George D. Mentz wrote the Alabama brief. In the oral argument, Mentz would speak before the justices in support of Jacob's side. Mentz's brief spoke strongly in favor of the right of state courts to be free from interference by federal courts. From the Alabama brief: "It is the essence of our federalism that states should have the widest latitude in the administration of their own systems of criminal justice."

The brief also spoke out strongly in favor of an indigent defendant's ability to effectively defend himself in criminal court: "At the last meeting of the Alabama Bar Association, there was widespread agreement among [prosecuting attorneys] that an accused, tried without aid of counsel, stands a better chance of obtaining from a jury either an outright acquittal or less severe punishment than one represented by an attorney."

This stood in stark contrast to Fortas's statement in the petitioner's brief that "There is no doubt that there is today widespread concensus among the states that legal assistance should be furnished to indigent persons."

The Alabama brief also countered Fortas's claim that *Betts* led to discrimination against poor people. Mentz wrote:

> The people of our United States have long . . .
> sought to avoid . . . a state of affairs in which the
> government takes care of the people. . . . [O]ur
> free enterprise system has always produced two
> classes of people—those who have and those who
> have not. No one questions the desirability of
> having furnished to those who are economically
> underprivileged many of the things which are
> available only to our more prosperous citizens. Yet
> it cannot be argued logically that a state's failure to

provide such things is a violation of the due process clause of the Fourteenth Amendment.

Finally, the Alabama brief countered a statement from the petitioner's brief that from 75 percent to 95 percent of all state criminal cases are decided by pleas of guilty, before a case can even go to trial. Fortas cited this statistic to support an assumption: that a great many indigent defendants plead guilty to a crime not because they really are guilty but in hopes of getting a lighter sentence. Here is how Mentz responded to that assumption:

> Surely, it is illogical, unwarranted and unrealistic to assume that, at most, anything more than a minute number of such guilty pleas are the product of anything other than a recognition by the accused that he is guilty . . . For such accused persons as do enter guilty pleas under these circumstances, can it be argued with reason that, if the accused is indigent, the state must be burdened with the necessity of appointing and paying an attorney solely for the purpose of pleading his client guilty?

THE TWENTY-TWO STATES' BRIEF

The briefs from North Carolina and Alabama were all the support Jacob would get. No other state attorney general responded to his call for support.

But to many people's surprise, twenty-two state attorneys general signed a brief strongly in support of the petitioner, calling for the Court to overturn *Betts*. A twenty-third state, Oregon, filed a separate brief. From the Twenty-Two-State Brief: "The undersigned Attorneys General . . . join in this brief amicus curiae in furtherance of a commonly held objective. That objective is to insure that every indigent person accused of any felony in a state court is guaranteed right of counsel. That right . . . is indispensable to the idea of justice under law."

The Twenty-Two States' brief made some of the same arguments that Fortas made in his brief. For example, on an indigent defendant's need for an attorney:

> Any trial, but particularly a criminal trial, is a highly complex, technical proceeding requiring representation by a trained legal adviser who can securely guide the accused through the maze of pitfalls into which he might otherwise stumble. The layman cannot, for instance, be expected to know procedure, whether to testify, how to cross-examine.

The brief had this to say about the effects on state courts if *Betts* were overturned: "The burden imposed upon the courts . . . by reconsideration of *Betts* v. *Brady* is manageable."

Here is how the brief ended:

> *Betts* v. *Brady*, already an anachronism when handed down, has spawned twenty years of bad law. That in the world of today a man may be condemned to penal servitude for lack of means to supply counsel for his defense is unthinkable. We respectfully urge that the conviction below [*Gideon* v. *Wainwright*] be reversed, that *Betts* v. *Brady* be reconsidered, and that this Court require that all persons tried for a felony in a state court shall have the right to counsel as a matter of due process of law and of equal protection of the laws.

THE ACLU BRIEF

The American Civil Liberties Union (ACLU) also submitted an amicus curiae brief in support of the petitioner.
This national organization is dedicated to defending
people's constitutional rights. The ACLU often submits
amicus curiae briefs in U.S. Supreme Court cases. The
brief's lead writer, J. Lee Rankin, would also speak on
behalf of the petitioner during the oral argument.

The brief announced the results of an ACLU survey of
state courts. The survey focused on the special circumstances provision of *Betts*. Since *Betts* was handed down,
139 cases were found where a state court could have
appointed a lawyer for an indigent defendant in a noncapital case due to special circumstances. How often did the
state courts actually appoint a lawyer?

In Pennsylvania, only once in 44 cases. In Maryland, 3
times out of 38. In Florida, 1 of 17. Altogether, in only 11 of
the 139 cases was an attorney actually appointed. The
other 128 indigent defendants were left to defend themselves.

When can a judge find special circumstances and
appoint an attorney? In most cases, this would happen
before the actual trial began. The judge would evaluate all
the special circumstances as they applied to the defendant
and appoint an attorney if he felt one was needed.

Or the judge could stop the trial at any time and
appoint an attorney. From the ACLU brief: "But no case
has been found in which a court, seeing the possibility of
unfairness during trial, has halted the proceeding so that
counsel could be appointed. Instead, courts permit the
unfair trial to run its course."

The brief also focused on the issue of poverty. It
reached back into U.S. history to show how people's atti-
tudes toward the poor had changed. From the ACLU
brief: "[I]n the early history of the Court the poor were

J. Lee Rankin wrote the ACLU's amicus curiae brief in support of Gideon's position.

stepchildren to the law, with limited rights and privileges." The brief cited a case from New York from 1837 in which the city court referred to "the moral pestilence of paupers."

The ACLU brief went on to state, "Although poverty is no longer equated with viciousness or with inferior status, the rule of *Betts* v. *Brady* persists as a grim reminder of the inequities of the past and as the law we are required to live by. The individuals in the state courts who are unable to secure counsel are ordinarily poor and without family. They are people who are least able to protect their personal liberty even when life imprisonment may be at stake." Finally, the brief stated that "The net effect of *Betts* v. *Brady* is to discriminate unfairly against criminal defendants who are poor."

Copies of all these briefs—petitioner's, respondent's, and the amicus curiae—were distributed to Fortas, to Jacob, and to the nine justices of the U.S. Supreme Court. The stage was set for the big event: oral argument.

eight

THE ORAL ARGUMENT

TO DECIDE a U.S. SUPREME COURT CASE, briefs are not enough. Imagine that you are a justice reading a brief and you have some doubts about a certain line of reasoning. You have questions. You need clarification. You could ask the brief a question, but it couldn't very well answer back. The people who wrote the briefs must be right there, face to face, to give you the answers you need. The most decisive and dramatic part of a U.S. Supreme Court case is the oral argument.

The *Gideon* v. *Wainwright* argument took place on January 15, 1963. Each side, petitioner and respondent, would have one hour to present their arguments, with an additional half-hour on each side for argument by a friend of the court.

Arguing the case for the petitioner were Abe Fortas of Arnold, Fortas & Porter, and J. Lee Rankin of the American Civil Liberties Union, amicus curiae. Arguing for the respondent were Bruce Jacob, assistant attorney general of the state of Florida, and George Mentz, assistant attorney general of the state of Alabama, amicus curiae.

The justices hearing the arguments for the petitioner and respondent, from the chief justice down through the ranks in order from oldest to newest member, were as follows:

Earl Warren, *Chief Justice of the United States*

Hugo L. Black, *Associate Justice*
William O. Douglas, *Associate Justice*
Tom C. Clark, *Associate Justice*
John M. Harlan, *Associate Justice*
William J. Brennan Jr., *Associate Justice*
Potter Stewart, *Associate Justice*
Byron R. White, *Associate Justice*
Arthur J. Goldberg, *Associate Justice*

The place was the U.S. Supreme Court Building at
1 First Street NE, Washington, D.C. As always, the courtroom stood open to the public on a first-come, first-
served basis. The room is impressive: marble columns
rising to a high ceiling with red velvet hangings and carved
horizontal bands of decoration along the walls.

THE SESSION BEGINS
As always, the session opens at 10 AM with the Court Crier
standing to the right of the bench, smashing a gavel on a
wooden block. At that point everyone in the room rises,
and the nine justices file in through red draperies behind
the bench. They stand in place as the Crier calls out: "The
Honorable, the Chief Justice, and the Associate Justices of
the Supreme Court of the United States. Oyez! Oyez!
Oyez!" This cry signals everyone to pay attention.

The Crier then continues, "All persons having business before the Honorable, the Supreme Court of the
United States, are admonished to draw near and give their
attention, for the Court is now sitting. God save the United
States and this Honorable Court!"

This completes the opening ritual. The argument is
now set to begin. The lawyers present their arguments
from two long tables set just below the long bench where
the justices sit. The Chief Justice sits in the center, with
the associate justices on alternating sides, based on their

seniority. The setting is surprisingly casual and informal for such a serious occasion. The lawyers speak in a conversational way. They do not look at a prepared text as they speak. Supreme Court rules state, "You should assume that all of the Justices have read the briefs filed in your case, including *amicus curiae* briefs. . . . Under no circumstances should you read your argument from a prepared script."

The lawyers are highly respectful of the justices throughout. The justices, on the other hand, are free to interrupt whenever they wish with comments and questions that can be challenging and argumentative. From the Supreme Court's "Guide for Counsel in Cases to Be Argued":

> *Never* interrupt a Justice who is addressing you. Give your full time and attention to that Justice— do not look down at your notes and do not look at your watch or at the clock located high on the wall behind the Justices. If you are speaking and a Justice interrupts you, cease talking immediately and listen.

Fortas Presents

Early in Fortas's hour, he talks about Gideon's trial for the poolroom break-in. From the oral argument:

> MR. FORTAS: Let me say this, if the Court please: If you will look at this transcript of the record [of Gideon's trial], perhaps you will share my feeling, which is a feeling of despondency.

Notice Fortas's show of respect here. His job is to sell his case, but not with hype and emotional pleas. He must be forceful, but he must ask, not demand, that the justices share his point of view based on facts and ideas that respectfully appeal to their intelligence. Fortas continues:

> This record does not indicate that Clarence Earl
> Gideon is a man of inferior natural talents. This
> record does not indicate that Clarence Earl
> Gideon is a moron or a person of low intelligence.
> This record does not indicate that the judge of the
> trial court in the State of Florida, or that the pros-
> ecuting attorney in the State of Florida, was
> derelict in his duty. On the contrary, it indicates
> that they tried to help Gideon.

Notice how Fortas begins three straight sentences
with "this record." His forceful repetition helps the justices see that the ideas in each sentence are linked. Notice
also how Fortas is building suspense. If the judge and
prosecuting attorney were trying to help his client, then
what is Fortas complaining about? In the next two sentences, he drives his point home:

> But to me, if the Court please, this record indicates
> the basic difficulty with *Betts* against *Brady*. And the
> basic difficulty with *Betts* against *Brady* is that no
> man, certainly no layman, can conduct a trial in his
> own defense so that the trial is a fair trial.

Now Justice John M. Harlan interrupts. Notice how
Fortas gets the justice himself to clarify the basic issue at
stake in the case.

> THE COURT [Justice Harlan]: Well, *Betts* and *Brady*
> did not proceed on that basis; it did not deny the
> obvious. Obviously, a man who is not represented
> . . . hasn't had as good a shake in court as the man
> who is represented. . . .

MR. FORTAS: Are you suggesting, Mr. Justice Harlan . . . that the real basis for *Betts* against *Brady* is the following: That a man does not get a fair trial if he is not represented by a lawyer, but that the demands of federalism over-weigh the absence of a fair trial?

THE COURT [Justice Harlan]: That's what I understood the basis of *Betts* and *Brady* to be, yes.

With the basic issue so clearly stated for the justices, Fortas can now explore it. Notice how he uses the point that Justice Harlan just made to help bolster his argument:

MR. FORTAS: I believe that this case dramatically illustrates the point that . . . a criminal court is not properly constituted . . . unless there is a judge and unless there is a counsel for the prosecution and unless there is a counsel for the defense. . . . [H]ow can we say . . . that a court is properly constituted, that a trial is fair, unless those conditions exist[?]

Fortas moves on to present the basic points from his brief, including the following argument: *Betts* has not worked out as planned. Defendants are hardly ever appointed an attorney due to special circumstances. But whenever an appeal based on *Betts* has reached the U.S. Supreme Court, the Court has always granted the appeal. Forty-five of the fifty states already appoint counsel for indigent defendants on a regular basis.

Fortas also mentions that attorneys general of twenty-two states have signed a brief urging the Court to overrule *Betts* v. *Brady*. One of the justices listening to the argument,

William O. Douglas, later wrote about the *Gideon* oral argument in his memoirs. He wrote that Fortas's presentation was "probably the best single legal argument" that he had heard in his thirty-six years on the Court. Fortas later became a Supreme Court justice himself.

rankin presents

Next, J. Lee Rankin of the ACLU has thirty minutes to present his argument in favor of the petitioner. Rankin is a lawyer and his argument is concise and direct. He begins: "Mr. Chief Justice, may it please the Court, the amici urge the Court to reconsider *Betts* against *Brady* and overrule it."

He then states the reason why: "[I]t is time, long passed, that our profession should stand up and say: We know because of our day-by-day experience that the ordinary layman can't get a fair trial, either in the Federal courts [of appeal] where it's corrected or in the State courts of this country where he represents himself."

Later, when Rankin repeats that a defendant cannot have a fair trial without counsel, Justice Harlan challenges him. Here is the exchange:

THE COURT [Justice Harlan]: That's a terribly broad generalization, Mr. Rankin.

MR. RANKIN: As a generalization, I think—

THE COURT [Justice Harlan]: There are many cases where . . . you would say that the best thing that a client could do . . . is to go in and try his case himself. . . . I'm not saying that there isn't force to your argument, but to make a sweeping generalization . . . that there can be no fair trial without a counsel ignores the facts of life that every lawyer knows.

Now Rankin must respond to the justice's challenge, keeping in mind that he must show respect for Harlan's disagreement without backing down:

MR. RANKIN: Mr. Justice Harlan, I'm trying to draw the distinction between the generalization in *Betts* against *Brady* that generally you can have a fair trial without counsel; that's what *Betts* against *Brady* says. And that only in special circumstances do you have an unfair trial without counsel. I say the rule has got to be turned around according to the facts; that generally you can't have a fair trial without counsel and the exception is the case that you and I know about where some skilled layman has been able to get a fair trial despite not having counsel. But *Betts* against *Brady* is built upon the premise that generally you can get a fair trial without counsel. And that's where I think it's unsound.

And so Rankin uses the justice's challenge as an opportunity to clarify his points about *Betts*, special circumstances, and fair trials.

Jacob presents

Now it's Bruce Jacob's turn. Remember that Jacob is only twenty-six, and this is his first argument before the Court. In this exchange with one of the justices, Jacob explains how state court judges decide whether an indigent defendant is capable of defending himself. (The justice's name is not given in the transcript of the oral argument, so he is identified only as "THE COURT.")

MR. JACOB: [Judges] spend perhaps 15, 20 minutes asking [the defendant] questions about his work experience, about his past history, his education, his experience in life, whether he's been convicted before and how much experience he's had in court; in other words, they try to follow the rules that have been set down by this Court in the cases since *Betts* versus *Brady*.

THE COURT: Well, is it assumed that a man who has been in jail a lot of times and been tried a lot of times becomes a lawyer from that? I would think that that group of people are probably about as little capable of taking care of themselves as any group you could get.

MR. JACOB: That circumstance in and of itself does not, of course—that circumstance in and of itself does not mean that a man can handle his own defense, but it certainly has a bearing on the question.

Note how the justice's comment forces Jacob to back down into a defensive position. From this exchange we get an idea of what a difficult job Jacob has taken on here. He must defend a ruling, *Betts*, which the justices themselves are criticizing.

In this next exchange, also about a defendant's ability to defend himself, we see the justices' sense of humor at work. We also see how Jacob's inexperience leads him to slip and say something he immediately regrets. (Note that when Jacob says, "No, it wouldn't," he really means yes, it would.)

THE COURT: I suppose I am right in my assumption I made earlier that Florida wouldn't permit Gideon or any other layman to defend anyone else in the State on trial, would it?

MR. JACOB: No, it wouldn't, Your Honor. Gideon could—if a man came into court and said, I want to be defended by Gideon, then certainly the court would not object.

THE COURT: It wouldn't?

THE COURT [another justice]: Wouldn't Gideon maybe get in trouble for practicing law without a license?

[Laughter]

THE COURT: With the local bar association.

MR. JACOB: I'm sorry, Your Honor; that was a stupid answer.

[Laughter]

Like Fortas, Jacob covers all the major points in his brief. As the two excerpts above show, he did not have an easy time defending a ruling—*Betts*—that was so unpopular.

MENTZ presents
Jacob gets some much-needed help from George D. Mentz, Alabama's assistant attorney general, who speaks on behalf of the respondent as a friend of the court. In his opening statement, Mentz gives a concise account of four of the respondent's five main points in favor of leaving *Betts* in place.

We contend that [1] the Sixth Amendment providing for representation by counsel in criminal prosecutions operates only on the Federal

Government; [2] that State appointment of counsel, in and of itself, is not an essential to a fair trial; [3] that an asserted denial of due process should be tested by an appraisal of the totality of the facts in a given case; and [4] that the Fourteenth Amendment's due process clause does not make the Sixth Amendment applicable to the States.

Then Mentz moves on to the fifth main point: the dollar cost to the states if *Betts* were overturned:

> The petitioner in this case has asserted that from 75 to 90 percent of all State cases are decided on pleas of guilty. . . . Practically everyone who pleads guilty to a criminal charge does so because he knows that the prosecuting authorities can prove his guilt and because he hopes to obtain leniency by dispensing with an unnecessary trial. And we say that a State should not be burdened with the expense of appointing an attorney who in good conscience could recommend only to his client that he enter a plea of guilty.

Shortly after this, Justice Harlan has a question for Mentz that helps uncover a weakness in the respondent's argument:

> THE COURT [Justice Harlan]: Can't you conceive of the possibility that many of these pleas of guilty are entered by people who, if advised by counsel, would have pleaded not guilty and might well have been acquitted?

> MR. MENTZ: Well, yes, sir, I admit that certain cases might turn that way; but on the other hand,

JUSTICE JOHN MARSHALL HARLAN WAS NAMED AFTER HIS GRANDFATHER, WHO SERVED ON THE SUPREME COURT FROM 1877 TO 1911.

my main contention is that by and large most of them would not. Of course, that's in the realm of speculation. I don't know, sir.

Thus Justice Harlan gets to the heart of what is wrong with *Betts*: That by denying counsel to indigent defendants, it influences the outcomes of cases—in favor of the State.

THE ARGUMENT ENDS

Much of Fortas's hour of argument is taken up by questions and comments from the justices. So they allow the attorney an extra five minutes at the end to sum up the case for the petitioner. In his remarks, Fortas mentions the issue of changing times:

> I think that *Betts* against *Brady* was wrong when decided; I think time has illuminated that fact. But I think that perhaps time has also done a service, because time has prepared the way so that the rule, the correct rule, the civilized rule, the rule of American constitutionalism, the rule of due process, may now be stated by this Court with minimum irritation and disruption in the States.

Justice Harlan then deals with the same issue from a different perspective, his own: "[W]hat one is left with is to get his hands on something that has happened between 1942 and 1963 that has made what the Court then regarded as constitutional suddenly become unconstitutional."

Here, Justice Harlan reveals his reluctance to vote to overrule *Betts*. We see how difficult it will be for him, and perhaps for other justices as well, to go against twenty years of precedent and make such a revolutionary change in U.S. law.

nine
THE RULING

AFTer reaDInG THe BrIeFs and hearing the oral arguments for each side, it was time for the justices to make up their minds. Would they rule for the petitioner and overturn *Betts* v. *Brady*? Or would they side with the respondent and let *Betts* stand?

Their decision would hinge on the way the justices saw the Fourteenth Amendment to the Constitution. Many parts of this enduring political document are deliberately general and vague. The Fourteenth Amendment is one of them. Does the amendment's due-process clause incorporate the Sixth Amendment right to an attorney in state criminal cases? That was a matter of interpretation.

Through the years the Court has made thousands of rulings, and each one has been influenced by the Court's makeup at the time: nine justices with nine different backgrounds, nine different personalities, and nine different ways of looking at the issues.

CONSTRUCTIONISTS versus ACTIVISTS

Justices are known by their records in past decisions. They are often categorized as either constructionist or activist, based on how freely they have interpreted the Constitution.

Constructionists tend to rely on the literal meaning of the actual words in the Constitution itself, rather than

THE U.S. SUPREME COURT JUSTICES WHO SERVED DURING THE *GIDEON* CASE. LEFT TO RIGHT, SEATED: ASSOCIATE JUSTICES TOM C. CLARK; HUGO L. BLACK; CHIEF JUSTICE EARL WARREN; WILLIAM O. DOUGLAS; AND JOHN M. HARLAN. STANDING: ASSOCIATE JUSTICES BYRON R. WHITE; WILLIAM J. BRENNAN JR.; POTTER STEWART; AND ARTHUR J. GOLDBERG.

trying to infer or imagine what the framers of the Constitution might have intended by those words. Constructionists tend to be cautious and conservative when it comes to interpreting the Constitution.

They also tend to favor judicial self-restraint. In many instances, constructionist justices would rather step back and let Congress or the states handle controversy. They also tend to be respectful of precedent and reluctant to overturn past rulings.

In the *Gideon* case, a strict constructionist might be more likely to rule against the petitioner. After all, the original intent of the Sixth Amendment was to protect defendants in federal courts only. Now Fortas, on behalf of Gideon, was asking the Court to expand that right to include felony crimes in state courts as well.

Activists, on the other hand, tend to be more liberal interpreters of the Constitution. They are less reluctant than constructionists to draw inferences from the words in the document, as long as those inferences reflect what they see as the Founding Fathers' vision of the United States of America.

Justice Hugo Black was known as an activist justice. To his way of thinking, the Founding Fathers were dedicated to protecting individual freedom from government oppression, and it was a justice's duty to do likewise. Sometimes this meant overruling precedent. Another justice, Oliver Wendell Holmes, issued this warning about being too respectful of precedent: "I believe that it is revolting to have no better reason for a rule of law than that it was laid down in the [past]. It is still more revolting if the grounds upon which it was laid down have vanished long since, and the rule simply persists from blind imitation of the past."

An activist justice might be more likely to rule in favor of the petitioner. After all, Fortas was asking the justices to overturn a twenty-year-old ruling that, in his view, was denying poor defendants rights that the Constitution guaranteed them.

THE MAKEUP OF THE COURT

How did this 1963 Court stack up in terms of constructionists versus activists? Fortas knew he could be certain of getting yes votes for overruling *Betts* from the Court's four activist justices: Chief Justice Earl Warren and Associate Justices Hugo Black, William O. Douglas, and William J. Brennan Jr. Justices Tom Clark, Potter Stewart, and Byron White were also likely yes votes.

So it looked as if the Court would vote to go against precedent and overturn *Betts* v. *Brady* by at least a 7 to 2 vote. Fortas thought that *Gideon* v. *Wainwright* deserved a complete victory, a 9 to 0 vote. That would depend on the votes of justices John M. Harlan and Arthur Goldberg. President John F. Kennedy had appointed Goldberg to the Court in August 1962, so Goldberg had been on the job only a few months. But as former Secretary of Labor, he was known to be more liberal-minded: another probable yes vote. That left only John M. Harlan, the Court's strictest constructionist, whose questions and comments during the oral argument revealed his reluctance to rule against precedent.

THE OPINIONS

On the first Friday after an oral argument, the justices hold a conference to vote on the case. Each justice casts a single vote for either the petitioner or respondent. The vote remains a secret until the majority opinion is completed. This written document, also known as the ruling, announces the Court's decision and explains the reasoning behind it.

Who is responsible for writing the majority opinion?

If the Chief Justice voted with the majority, he assigns the task to himself or to one of the other majority justices. If not, the choosing is done by the senior justice on the majority side, the one with the most years of active service on the Court.

The minority members usually agree on a justice to write a dissenting opinion, explaining why they disagree with the majority. Also, any individual justice is free to write his or her own dissenting opinion, or an opinion that agrees with the majority, known as a concurring opinion.

Though it will be credited to a single author, the majority opinion is a cooperative effort. U.S. Supreme Court rulings tend to be tens of thousands of words long and weeks and sometimes months in the making. The opinion will be researched, discussed, drafted, and rewritten several times before all the majority justices can agree on the exact wording. During that time, justices may change their minds about certain issues and even switch sides.

Day of Decision

Chief Justice Warren chose Justice Black to author the majority opinion. The choice was appropriate, since Black had played vital parts in precedent-setting cases leading up to *Gideon*. President Franklin D. Roosevelt appointed Black to the Court in 1937. Black authored majority opinions in *Johnson* v. *Zerbst* (1938) and *Griffin* v. *Illinois* (1956). Black also wrote a strongly worded dissent in *Betts* v. *Brady*.

On Monday, March 18, 1963, Black announced the Court's decision in the case of *Gideon* v. *Wainwright*. All in all, the justices wrote four opinions: Black's majority opinion and concurring opinions by Clark, Douglas, and Harlan. There were no dissenting opinions because there were no dissenting votes. Even strict constructionist John

naming cases

Cases like Gideon's use this naming pattern: Petitioner versus Respondent. The petitioner is the prisoner attempting to have his conviction overturned. But the respondent is not an individual; it is the entire prison system of the state. Calling the case *Gideon v. the Florida State Prison System* would make for a long and unwieldy title. So to shorten and simplify it, the last name of the head of the state's prison system is used in the respondent's place.

When the Gideon case began, the state prison system was headed by H. G. Cochran Jr., director of the Florida Division of Corrections. So the case was known as *Gideon v. Cochran*. During the appeals process, Cochran resigned. His replacement, Louie L. Wainwright, took his place as respondent and thus lent his name to a landmark case in U.S. judicial history.

M. Harlan joined the majority. The Court had overturned *Betts v. Brady* by a 9 to 0 vote.

Justice Black announced the decision from the bench, along with the other eight justices, in the Supreme Court room. In a biography of Justice Black, Roger Newman describes the moment this way: "When [Chief Justice] Warren called on him on the bench, [Black] leaned forward and spoke in an almost folksy way, reading sections of his opinion. Happiness, contentment, gratification filled his voice."

THE DECISION

Justice Black's opinion in *Gideon* focuses on two clauses from the Fourteenth Amendment. One, the due-process clause, is about getting a fair trial. The other, the equal-protection clause, is about equal justice for all persons, rich and poor alike. Both clauses are about protecting the individual from the power of the government.

Early on, Justice Black's opinion refers to *Betts* v. *Brady*: "Since 1942, when *Betts* v. *Brady* was decided by a divided Court, the problem of a defendant's federal constitutional right to counsel in a state court has been a continuing source of controversy and litigation in both state and federal courts. To give this problem another review here, we granted certiorari."

Then, after linking *Gideon* with *Betts*, Black announces the Court's decision: "Since the facts and circumstances of the two cases are so nearly indistinguishable, we think the *Betts* v. *Brady* holding if left standing would require us to reject Gideon's claim that the Constitution guarantees him the assistance of counsel. Upon full reconsideration we conclude that *Betts* v. *Brady* should be overruled."

With this announcement, two sections of the U.S. Constitution had been reinterpreted. When it came to criminal trials, the Sixth and the Fourteenth Amendments now applied to state courts as well as the federal courts. The opinion then tells how the Court came to this decision:

> We accept *Betts* v. *Brady*'s assumption, based as it
> was on our prior cases, that a provision of the Bill
> of Rights which is "fundamental and essential to a
> fair trial" is made obligatory upon the States by the
> Fourteenth Amendment.

> We think the Court in *Betts* was wrong, however, in

concluding that the Sixth Amendment's guarantee
of counsel is not one of these fundamental rights.

That is, the Court in *Betts* agreed that no court could tell
a defendant he may not hire an attorney to represent him.
But, *Betts* said, that did not mean that a state court had to
hire an attorney for the defendant if he could not afford
to pay for one. The *guarantee* of counsel was limited to
indigent criminal defendants in federal courts. It did not
apply to defendants in state criminal courts. This, the
Gideon opinion says, is where Betts went seriously wrong.

DUE PROCESS: THE RIGHT TO COUNSEL

Justice Black then looks back at precedent to show how the
Court's opinions on the due-process right to counsel have
changed over the years. He begins with *Powell* v. *Alabama*:

> Ten years before *Betts* v. *Brady*, this Court [in
> *Powell*]. . . had unequivocally declared that "the
> right to the aid of counsel is of this fundamental
> character." While the Court at the close of its
> *Powell* opinion did . . . limit its holding to the par-
> ticular facts and circumstances of that case, its
> conclusions about the fundamental nature of the
> right to counsel are unmistakable.

That is, while the Court in *Powell* (1932) limited the
right to counsel in state courts to capital cases, the Court
called it a fundamental constitutional right for *all* defendants. Here, Black is saying that in our system of justice,
when a defendant unskilled in legal matters is matched
against a professional prosecuting attorney, the defendant must have his own attorney. Otherwise he will have
little or no chance of presenting an effective defense.

HUGO L. BLACK WAS APPOINTED TO THE SUPREME COURT IN 1937 BY PRESIDENT FRANKLIN DELANO ROOSEVELT. HE WROTE THE MAJORITY DECISION IN THE *GIDEON* V. *WAINWRIGHT* CASE.

POVERTY AND EQUAL PROTECTION

In another part of the opinion, Justice Black focuses on the issues of poverty and equal protection: "Not only these precedents but also reason and reflection require us to recognize that in our adversary system of criminal justice, any person haled into court, who is too poor to hire a

JUSTICE BLACK'S BACKGROUND

Justice Hugo L. Black's early career in criminal justice demonstrates a long-standing concern for making sure that defendants are properly represented in courts of law. Before becoming a justice, Black was a lawyer, a prosecutor, and a judge. He knew what life was like on all sides of the legal system. As a defense lawyer, he represented African-American prisoners who were kept in jail long after they should have been released. As a prosecutor, he opposed police who used violent tactics to force suspects to confess.

Justice Black's past also shows a concern for the poor and disadvantaged. As a lawyer, he represented coal miners in rural Alabama who were on strike for higher wages. As a prosecutor, he opposed insurance companies when they refused to give workers a fair monetary settlement for injuries suffered on the job.

Together, these concerns show just how strongly Justice Black felt about protecting disadvantaged defendants. To his way of thinking, denying a poor defendant counsel was both unfair and unconstitutional.

lawyer, cannot be assured a fair trial unless counsel is provided for him. This seems to us to be an obvious truth."

Justice Black goes on to explain why this should be an obvious truth:

Governments, both state and federal, quite properly spend vast sums of money to establish

machinery to try defendants accused of crime.
Lawyers to prosecute are everywhere deemed
essential to protect the public's interest in an
orderly society. Similarly, there are few defendants charged with crime, few indeed, who fail to
hire the best lawyers they can get to prepare and
present their defenses. That government hires
lawyers to prosecute and defendants who have the
money hire lawyers to defend are the strongest
indications of the widespread belief that lawyers
in criminal courts are necessities, not luxuries.
The right of one charged with crime to counsel
may not be deemed fundamental and essential to
fair trials in some countries, but it is in ours. . . .
Our state and national constitutions and laws have
laid great emphasis on procedural and substantive
safeguards designed to assure fair trials before
impartial tribunals in which every defendant
stands equal before the law. This noble idea
cannot be realized if the poor man charged with
crime has to face his accusers without a lawyer to
assist him.

The majority opinion ends by returning to *Betts* v.
Brady:

The Court in *Betts* v. *Brady* departed from the
sound wisdom upon which the Court's holding in
Powell v. *Alabama* rested. Florida, supported by
two other States, has asked that *Betts* v. *Brady* be
left intact. Twenty-two States, as friends of the
Court, argue that *Betts* was "an anachronism when
handed down" and that it should now be overruled. We agree. The judgment is reversed and the
cause is remanded to the Supreme Court of

Florida for further action not inconsistent with this opinion.

Finally, what about John M. Harlan, the Court's strict constructionist and least likely member to vote to overturn *Betts*? How did he feel about his decision to vote against precedent? In his concurring opinion, Harlan wrote: "The special circumstances rule has been formally abandoned in capital cases, and the time has now come when it should be similarly abandoned in noncapital cases. . . . This indeed does no more than to make explicit something that has long since been foreshadowed in our decisions."

ten
REACTIONS

THE U.S. supreme court had finished its job. Now it was up to the rest of the criminal justice system to see to it that indigent defendants in state criminal courts had access to lawyers who could effectively defend them.

That meant that lawmakers, criminal court judges, and defense attorneys had work to do. Fortunately, most states had done the work. They already had systems in place for providing counsel. Now it was up to the remaining five states to respond. They had these basic options to choose from: set up a public defender's office, publish an approved list of defense lawyers for judges to choose from, or leave it entirely up to judges to appoint attorneys on a case-by-case basis.

CHOOSING OPTIONS
The public defender option went like this: Individual cities, counties, and judicial districts would set up local public defender's offices. They would be staffed by professional defense lawyers paid by the state to represent indigent defendants. This option was attractive because public defenders are devoted entirely to the field of criminal law.

Most lawyers specialize in one field of law or another. Some work in real estate law or tax law. Others work in divorce law, zoning law, or some other field. Each field has its own complex and ever-changing set of laws.

Lawyers who specialize in a field other than criminal law cannot be expected to be experts at defending clients in criminal cases.

Public defenders, on the other hand, can match prosecutors in all the vital areas of criminal defense. They know criminal law. They are familiar with the judges in the criminal court system. They know how to go about selecting juries and presenting cases to them. They know the strategies that prosecuting attorneys use and how to counteract those strategies.

The state of Florida, where Gideon was tried, chose the public defender option. In May 1963, only two months after the *Gideon* ruling was handed down, the Florida legislature passed a public defender plan. Each of the state's sixteen judicial districts would get its own public defender's office, which would appoint lawyers from its staff to represent indigent defendants.

The other four states, North Carolina, Alabama, Mississippi, and South Carolina, set up systems for court-appointed lawyers. The North Carolina legislature assigned the state bar association and state supreme court to set down rules for guiding judges in assigning lawyers. The North Carolina legislature also set aside $500,000 to get its system going. The legislatures of Alabama, Mississippi, and South Carolina set up similar systems for court-appointed lawyers.

progress report

Within months of *Gideon's* passage, all fifty states had an organized system in place for supplying counsel for indigent defendants. Florida lawmakers even went a step further. They voted to apply *Gideon* retroactively to all criminal defendants. That meant that everyone in prison convicted of a felony when they were not represented by counsel was now in the same position as Gideon himself:

Their convictions were reversed.

By January 1, 1964, nearly one thousand prisoners had been set free for good. They would not be tried again because Florida state authorities doubted that they could get a conviction a second time. Another five hundred prisoners would be retried, while authorities were looking at habeas corpus petitions from hundreds more.

All this progress coming so fast made the *Gideon* ruling appear to be a spectacular success. And looking back beyond *Powell*, it certainly was. Before 1932 the U.S. Constitution left the actions of state law enforcement officers virtually unchecked. The chances of the U.S. Supreme Court reversing any conviction in a state criminal court were nearly nonexistent.

Then came *Powell*, and little by little the Court began applying the due process and equal protection clauses of the Fourteenth Amendment to state criminal courts. Now, with *Gideon*, it looked as if the struggle for the right to counsel was over at last.

Newspapers published the news with a mixture of outrage over past wrongs and joy over *Gideon* correcting those wrongs. From an editorial in the *Washington Post*: "It is intolerable in a nation which proclaims equal justice under law as one of its ideals that anyone should be handicapped in defending himself simply because he happens to be poor."

From an editorial in Florida, the *St. Petersburg Times*: "Most persons, we are sure, will be thankful that the Supreme Court clings to the ancient democratic tradition of protecting the individual against the tyranny of any governmental agency."

Miranda v. Arizona

This trend toward protecting the individual from government power continued. Just three years after the *Gideon* ruling, the Court widened the right of counsel once again. The case was *Miranda* v. *Arizona* (1966).

Miranda extended the right to counsel in two important ways. First, there was the time factor. *Gideon* had guaranteed a criminal *defendant* the right to an attorney. *Miranda* extended that right to a criminal *suspect* when the Court ruled that the right to counsel began at the very moment that a law officer places a person under arrest.

Second, there was the factor of a verbal warning. The arresting officer now had to tell the suspect, as he was being arrested, that he had the right to an attorney. The Miranda warning goes like this:

- You have the right to remain silent.
- Anything you say can and will be used against you in a court of law.
- You have the right to talk to a lawyer and have him present with you during questioning.
- If you cannot afford a lawyer, one will be appointed to represent you.
- Do you understand each of these rights as I have explained them to you?
- Having these rights in mind, do you wish to talk to us now?

The following passage from the *Miranda* ruling explains why the Court decided that the right to an attorney had to be widened from where *Gideon* had left it:

In order fully to apprise a person interrogated of the extent of his rights under this system then, it is necessary to warn him not only that he has the right to consult with an attorney, but also that if he is indigent a lawyer will be appointed to represent him. Without this additional warning, the

---

WARNING AS TO YOUR RIGHTS

You are under arrest. Before we ask you any questions, you must understand what your rights are.

You have the right to remain silent. You are not required to say anything to us at any time or to answer any questions. Anything you say can be used against you in court.

You have the right to talk to a lawyer for advice before we question you and to have him with you during questioning.

If you cannot afford a lawyer and want one, a lawyer will be provided for you.

If you want to answer questions now without a lawyer present you will still have the right to stop answering at any time. You also have the right to stop answering at any time until you talk to a lawyer.   P. 1175

POLICE OFFICERS CARRY A CARD WITH THE MIRANDA WARNING TO READ ALOUD TO SUSPECTS AS THEY ARREST THEM.

admonition of the right to consult with counsel would often be understood as meaning only that he can consult with a lawyer if he has one or has the funds to obtain one. The warning of a right to counsel would be hollow if not couched in terms that would convey to the indigent—the person most often subjected to interrogation—the knowledge that he too has a right to have counsel present.

unanswered questions

The *Gideon* ruling was greeted with acclaim, but it was not perfect. It left behind unanswered questions. The *Miranda* ruling answered one of these questions: At what stage in a criminal case does the defendant's right to counsel kick in?

But other questions remained. The *Gideon* ruling made it clear that the right to counsel applied to defendants accused of felonies. But what about less serious crimes? Did an indigent defendant accused of a misdemeanor have a right to counsel too? And what about persons who were already serving time in prison after being convicted in trials where they had to defend themselves? The state of Florida reversed their convictions, but what about prisoners in other states?

And finally, what about the lawyers who would now be representing indigent defendants in criminal trials? *Gideon* said that states had to provide lawyers, but it did not say that these lawyers had to be experienced in criminal law, and it did not say how much money the states should set aside to pay these lawyers. That would be up to state lawmakers to determine.

So, how would the states handle their new responsibilities? How effective would this landmark U.S. Supreme Court ruling known as *Gideon* v. *Wainwright* prove to be in the years to come?

eleven
GIDEON TODAY

In 2003, forty years after the *Gideon* ruling, people involved in the case looked back. One was reporter and author Anthony Lewis, who covered *Gideon* v. *Wainwright* for the *New York Times* and wrote a best-selling book about the case called *Gideon's Trumpet.*

Speaking of how he felt in 1963, Lewis said: "After the Supreme Court decision, I recognized that it would be, as I wrote then, 'an enormous social task to bring to life the dream of *Gideon* v. *Wainwright*—the dream of a vast, diverse country in which every man charged with crime will be capably defended . . . sure of the support needed to make an adequate defense.'"

And how well did the nation's criminal justice system do bringing this dream to life? Abe Krash, a member of Arnold, Fortas & Porter, helped Fortas put the case together. Looking back forty years, he said:

> It is true that the high hopes entertained by Fortas and Black in 1963 have not been completely ful-filled. At the time, many of us did not fully appre-ciate that it is not enough to guarantee that a defendant has a lawyer at his side; the critical questions are whether that lawyer is qualified to try a criminal case, and whether the accused has the financial resources to conduct an investigation

and to retain expert witnesses. Much remains to be done if the right to counsel is to be made meaningful.

Forty years earlier, in his respondent's brief, Bruce Jacob focused on the same potential problem. From the brief:

> An automatic requirement that counsel be appointed in every case would not decrease the quantity of habeas corpus petitions being filed in federal courts. The trend in habeas corpus petitions is to allege lack of *adequate* representation, and this problem will not be solved by imposition of a rule requiring automatic appointment.

Reading this passage from Jacob's brief of 1962, it's almost as if he were looking into the future. Getting a lawyer for an indigent defendant was one thing. Getting a competent, experienced criminal lawyer has proved to be quite another.

THe sLeePInG LawYer

How serious was the problem of getting a competent criminal lawyer? Take the case of Calvin J. Burdine. In 1984, Burdine was convicted in Texas of murder and sentenced to death. In 2002 he won the right to a new trial. Why? Because Joe Frank Cannon, his court-appointed lawyer, could not seem to stay awake. Several times during the trial, Cannon was observed falling asleep at the defense table.

The United States Court of Appeals granted Burdine the new trial. But the vote was not unanimous. Five of the fourteen judges on the panel voted against him. Lewis wrote: "That is, five of those distinguished federal judges

CALVIN BURDINE EVENTUALLY PLED GUILTY TO MURDER AND IS SERVING A
LIFE SENTENCE.

thought a lawyer who fell asleep during a capital trial did not do enough harm to matter."

What happened to Cannon after he was discovered sleeping on the job as his client's life was at stake? We might think that would be the last time he would be appointed to defend an indigent man. But Lewis wrote: "Calvin Burdine's lawyer, Joe Frank Cannon, was appointed by judges in Houston to other cases after he slept through Burdine's trial. In Texas and other places, some appointments of counsel are regarded as sinecures [jobs that require little or no real work] to be given to friends and supporters."

And Cannon was not the only sleeping lawyer to defend an indigent man on trial for his life. A Houston, Texas, newspaper reporter wrote this about another court-appointed lawyer in a capital trial: "His mouth kept falling open and his head lolled back on his shoulders, and then he awakened just long enough to catch himself and sit upright. Then it happened again. And again. And again."

EFFECTIVE LEGAL AID

In his petitioner's brief, Abe Fortas also argued for effective legal representation. He wrote that the states should "guarantee effective legal aid to all persons accused of a serious offense who do not competently and intelligently waive such assistance."

And just what is effective legal aid? Obviously it's not a lawyer who sleeps through the trial or who sees his defense duties as a job demanding little or no work. Instead, it's a lawyer who can help the defendant understand the charges against him, how to testify, and when to remain silent. It's a lawyer who knows how to file motions, how to examine prospective jurors, when to make objections, and how to perform all the many other crucial skills that go into defending someone accused of a crime.

But Fortas's argument for effective legal aid never made its way into the *Gideon* ruling. Kim Taylor-Thompson is a law professor at the New York University School of Law who has researched and written about this issue. She writes:

> The Court simply elected not to explore in any depth those attributes of representation that the accused is constitutionally guaranteed in a criminal prosecution. That omission has contributed to the all too common practice of jurisdictions tolerating and even fostering minimal levels of performance by counsel appointed to represent indigent clients in criminal cases.

Money Problems

If the Court had explored the attributes of a good defense lawyer in its ruling, today's problems with legal representation would be less serious. In its *Gideon* opinion, the Court never even mentioned the most serious problem of all: money. In order to retain the services of effective criminal defense lawyers, the states must pay them a reasonable amount of money. Do they?

Taylor-Thompson writes about the tendency of state legislatures who decide how tax money is spent to "conduct volume business at rock-bottom prices." She writes that these funding authorities demand that public defenders and court-appointed lawyers "handle at discounted prices a set number of cases during a . . . year."

This reluctance to spend more also means that public defender offices cannot provide the kind of training that lawyers need to keep up with the changes in criminal law. The result, Taylor-Thompson says, is "loss in quality."

How do the lawyers themselves feel? William J. Leahy, chief counsel of the Massachusetts Association of

Criminal Defense Lawyers, spoke about what he calls a crisis in his field of law. The following is from a speech he delivered to mark the fortieth anniversary of *Gideon* v. *Wainwright*:

> It is most important to emphasize that this is not a crisis of . . . poor lawyering, or any lack of zeal. No, the right to counsel in Massachusetts is today in excellent condition, in every respect but one. We have a capable and public-spirited cadre of attorneys who serve the public interest by representing the poor with competence and passion; we have an agency which takes seriously its responsibility to provide high quality representation; we have training expectations and performance standards which meet or exceed every comparison. We simply do not have enough money! Or, to be more precise, we do not receive sufficient funding to pay a reasonable hourly rate to assigned private counsel, or reasonable salaries to our staff attorneys.

What is a reasonable rate of pay for a criminal defense attorney? Private defense attorneys routinely charge more than two hundred dollars an hour. They are paid by their individual clients. Compare that with the hourly rate that states routinely pay. Court-appointed lawyers who work for Suffolk Lawyers for Justice (SLJ) in New York state are paid between thirty and forty-five dollars an hour.

In addition to his private practice and part-time work as a professor at Harvard Law School, John Salsberg also does work for the SLJ. He says: "There are an awful lot of wonderful lawyers who do this court-appointed work, and I think a lot of them will do less and less of it, leaving the work to less experienced people."

The money problem is especially severe in capital cases. Mike Ramsey is a criminal defense attorney in Houston, Texas, who specializes in capital crimes. He says that there is not enough money available to pay court-appointed lawyers in capital cases a reasonable wage. The result? "In Houston, there are probably 20 lawyers who are qualified to represent capital defendants. In 50 percent of the cases, we get time-servers, people who are holding their [defendants'] hands on the way to the death chamber."

Professor Kim Taylor-Thompson sums up the joy and disappointment of *Gideon* v. *Wainwright* this way:

With the stroke of a pen, the Court converted this landscape by mandating the appointment of counsel to advocate for the individual accused of a crime in state courts. In that instant, the Supreme Court reshaped the system of justice in state criminal trials. Or so it seemed. For all its significance, the *Gideon* decision has fallen short of the goal the Court seemed intent on achieving.

twelve
Gideon's Fate

WHAT ABOUT CLARENCE EARL GIDEON himself? *Gideon* v. *Wainwright* declared that "The judgment is reversed and the cause is remanded to the Supreme Court of Florida for further action not inconsistent with this opinion."

The further action turned out to be a retrial. Gideon would be tried once again for the poolroom break-in. But this time he would have a lawyer.

Gideon's reaction to all this was despair. The judge who tried him the first time, Judge Robert L. McCrary Jr., would be trying him again. Gideon did not believe he would receive a fair trial this time either, even with a court-appointed attorney.

GIDEON'S CHOICE
It looked like Gideon would have no trouble finding a good defense attorney. The ACLU offered to supply a pair of experienced criminal lawyers to defend him free of charge. They would be among the best attorneys in the entire nation.

To many people's surprise, Gideon turned down the ACLU's offer. Clarence Earl Gideon was not an easy person to deal with. He had always been a nonconformist. He had spent his life as a drifter and a habitual small-time criminal. He did not know much about how the everyday world worked and he did not always think things through clearly. But for all that, Clarence Earl Gideon was a decisive man. He knew who he did not want to defend him: the ACLU lawyers. And he knew who he did want: W. Fred Turner.

Turner accepted the job, but right away he realized that defending Gideon would not be easy. Gideon ordered him to make several motions. One was to have the site of the trial changed from Panama City, Florida, to the state's capital, Tallahassee.

Turner told Gideon that this would not be a good idea. Turner was a local criminal lawyer who knew most of the people in the small town of Panama City, including many who would be in the jury pool. Finally, Gideon agreed. Then Turner delivered an ultimatum: "I'll only represent you if you will stop trying to be the lawyer and let me handle the case." And again, Gideon agreed.

jury selection

Clarence Earl Gideon's retrial for the Bay Harbor poolroom break-in began at 9 AM, August 5, 1963. The first step was jury selection. The pool consisted of twenty-eight men, from whom a jury of six would be selected. Turner and William E. Harris, the assistant state attorney prosecuting the case, would do the selecting.

Turner's knowledge and experience in criminal law came into play right away as he dismissed the first two jurors approved by Harris. Turner knew that one of the men did not approve of people who drank alcohol, as Gideon did. And the second one Turner recognized, from past trials, as a person whom lawyers classified as a convicter: a person who tended to believe that a person charged with a crime was guilty even if the evidence pointed in the other direction.

What a change this was from the first trial. Defending

himself, Gideon had not questioned any potential jurors, and he had blindly accepted the six chosen by the prosecuting attorney.

DAMAGING TESTIMONY

After the jury was selected, the prosecution presented its case, and Turner went to work. One key prosecution witness was Preston Bray, the cab driver who gave Gideon a ride on the morning of the break-in. As he had in the first trial, Bray testified that Gideon told him not to say anything about picking him up that morning.

During the first trial, Gideon had let this damaging bit of testimony go unchallenged. But this time, Turner asked Bray a question: Had Gideon ever said anything like that to him before?

Bray answered yes, Gideon said something like that every time he called a cab. "Why?" Turner asked.

"I understand it was his wife," Bray answered. "He had trouble with his wife."

Just like that, with a few simple questions, Turner managed to make Bray's damaging testimony harmless. But the witness with the most damaging testimony of all was Henry Cook.

THE STATE'S STAR WITNESS

At the first trial, it was Cook's eyewitness testimony that put Gideon at the scene of the crime. Cook had testified that he saw Gideon walk out of the poolroom that morning, shortly before he, Cook, went inside and discovered the break-in.

In the weeks before that first trial, Gideon was locked away in a prison cell, under arrest. Without a lawyer to represent him, Gideon could not possibly have done what Turner did during the weeks before the second trial. Turner checked out the criminal record of Henry Cook.

Turner also traveled to Panama City, the scene of the crime, and did some investigating. He saw what the pool-room and the surrounding streets looked like. He saw where the pay phone was located. He saw where Henry Cook said he and his friends were waiting for the pool-room to open. And from what he learned and saw, Turner drew some interesting conclusions.

When Cook took the stand, Turner knew the right questions to ask. In his cross-examination, Turner asked Cook about his criminal record. He asked Cook what he and his friends were doing that morning outside the pool-room an hour and a half before it was due to open. He asked Cook why he did not immediately call police that morning to tell them about the break-in and Gideon's presence at the crime scene. Turner's questions strongly suggested that Cook and his friends, not Gideon, were responsible for the break-in.

Turner got Cook to admit that he was a convicted felon who had been convicted of stealing a car. He did not get Cook to admit that he, not Gideon, was the person responsible for the break-in. But he did succeed in casting plenty of doubt on the character of the prosecution's star witness.

THE RIGHT DECISION

In his closing argument, Turner told the jury that Gideon was innocent. He said that what actually happened was this: Cook's friends were inside the poolroom robbing it, with Cook acting as the lookout man, when Gideon happened along. Cook had accused Gideon of the burglary, Turner said, to divert suspicion from himself and his friends.

Testimony was concluded by 3 PM that same day. The jury needed only an hour to return with their decision. This time the verdict was not guilty.

CLARENCE EARL GIDEON CELEBRATES HIS NEWFOUND FREEDOM BY SHOOTING A GAME OF POOL AT THE BAY HARBOR POOLROOM IN PANAMA CITY.

In a letter to Bruce Jacob, as Jacob was preparing the respondent's brief, Judge McCrary explained why he had denied Gideon a lawyer at the first trial. McCrary wrote:

> [Gideon] was advised that when a person appears to have the mental ability to interview witnesses and present testimony to the jury, the practice of appointing counsel is not followed except in capital cases. After talking with this defendant, it was my opinion that he had both the mental capacity and the experience in the courtroom at previous trials to adequately conduct his defense. This was later borne out at the trial, as you can determine from examination of the record in this case.

But the results of the second trial had proven otherwise. Looking at how Gideon had conducted his defense versus how Turner had conducted it was like the difference between night and day. Gideon's two trials provided proof positive that in *Gideon* v. *Wainwright*, the nine justices of the U.S. Supreme Court had made the right decision.

A MILESTONE

When all is said and done, what does *Gideon* v. *Wainwright* tell us about the law? Abe Krash, who helped Abe Fortas prepare the Gideon case, wrote: "The right to counsel in a criminal prosecution is acknowledged to be a fundamental right. The *Gideon* case stands as a milestone in American constitutional law because it affirms a principle that is basic in a free and just society."

And here is what Attorney General Robert F. Kennedy had to say about Gideon on November 1, 1963:

> If an obscure Florida convict named Clarence Earl Gideon had not sat down in his prison cell with a

ATTORNEY GENERAL ROBERT F. KENNEDY PRAISED CLARENCE EARL GIDEON IN 1963. HERE, HE IS SEEN GREETING SCHOOLCHILDREN IN 1965, WHEN HE WAS A U.S. SENATOR.

pencil and paper to write a letter to the Supreme
Court, and if the Supreme Court had not taken the
trouble to look for merit in that one crude petition
among all the bundles of mail it must receive every
day, the vast machinery of American law would
have gone on functioning undisturbed.

But Gideon *did* write that letter, the Court *did* look
into his case, he *was* retried with the help of a competent
defense counsel, found not guilty, and released from
prison after two years of punishment for a crime he did
not commit—and the whole course of American legal history has been changed.

Clarence Earl Gideon died on January 18, 1972. On his
gravestone are carved words he had written to Abe Fortas
before his case was argued before the Supreme Court:
"Each era finds an improvement in law for the benefit of
mankind."

CLARENCE EARL GIDEON'S GRAVESTONE AT MOUNT OLIVET CEMETERY IN
HANNIBAL, MISSOURI.

NOTES

Chapter 1

p. 14, par. 4, *Gideon* v. *Wainwright*, 372 U.S. 335 (1963). http://caselaw.lp.findlaw.com/scripts/getcase.pl?court =us&vol=372&invol=335

p. 14, par. 5, Motion to Proceed in Forma Pauperis and Petition for Writ of Certiorari. http://www.nacdl.org/public.nsf/GideonAnniversary/ pleadings?opendocument

p. 16, par. 1, Response to Petition for Writ of Certiorari, State of Florida. http://www.nacdl.org/public.nsf/GideonAnniversary/ pleadings?opendocument

p. 16, par. 3, Response to Petition for Writ of Certiorari, State of Florida.

p. 17, par. 1, Answer to Response to Petition for Writ of Certiorari. http://www.nacdl.org/public.nsf/Gideon Anniversary/pleadings?opendocument

p. 19, par. 1, Lewis, Anthony. *Gideon's Trumpet*. New York: Random House, 1964, p. 27.

p. 19, par. 3, Rules of the Supreme Court of the United States. http://www.law.cornell.edu/rules/supct/10.html

Chapter 2

p. 27, par. 4, Lewis, Anthony. *Gideon's Trumpet*. New York: Random House, 1964, p. 65.

p. 28, par. 6, Lewis, *Gideon's Trumpet*, p. 69.

p. 30, par. 4, Lewis, p. 81.

p. 30, par. 6, Lewis, p. 81.

Sidebar

p. 35, The Magna Carta (The Great Charter) http://www.
cs.indiana.edu/statecraft/magna-carta.html

Chapter 3

p. 37, par. 3, *Powell* v. *State of Alabama*, 287 U.S. 45
(1932). Findlaw.com. http://caselaw.lp.findlaw.com/
scripts/getcase.pl?court=US&vol=287&invol=45

p. 37, par. 4, *Powell*, 287 U.S. 45 (1932).

p. 38, par. 1, *Powell*.

p. 38, par. 3, *Powell*.

p. 38, par. 4, *Powell*.

p. 39, par. 1, *Powell*.

p. 40, par. 2, *Brown* v. *Board of Education*, 347 U.S. 483
(1954). http://www.nationalcenter.org/brown.html

p. 42, par. 1, *Johnson* v. *Zerbst*, 304 U.S. 458 (1938).
http://caselaw.lp.findlaw.com/scripts/getcase.pl?court
=US&vol=304&invol=458

p. 42, par. 3, *Johnson* v. *Zerbst*, 304 U.S. 458 (1938).

Chapter 4

p. 44, par. 1, *Gideon* v. *Wainwright*, 372 U.S. 335 (1963).
http://caselaw.lp.findlaw.com/scripts/getcase.pl?court
=us&vol=372&invol=335

p. 45, par. 3, *Powell* v. *State of Alabama*, 287 U.S. 45
(1932). Findlaw.com. http://caselaw.lp.findlaw.com/
scripts/getcase.pl?court=US&vol=287&invol=45

p. 45, par. 4, *Betts* v. *Brady*, 316 U.S. 455 (1942)
http://caselaw.lp.findlaw.com/cgi-bin/getcase.pl?court
=us&vol=316&invol=455

p. 45, par. 6–p. 46, par. 1, *Betts*, 316 U.S. 455 (1942).

p. 46, par. 2, *Betts.*
p. 46, par. 3, *Betts.*
p. 47, par. 2, *Betts.*
p. 48, par. 1, *Betts.*

Chapter 5

p. 49, par. 2, *Uveges* v. *Commonwealth of Pennsylvania*, 355
U.S. 437 (1948). http://caselaw.lp.findlaw.com/scripts/
getcase.pl?court=us&vol=335&invol=437
p. 50, par. 1, Uveges, 355 U.S. 437 (1948).
p. 50, par. 5–p. 51, par. 1, *McNeal* v. *Culver*, 365 U.S. 109
(1961). http://caselaw.lp.findlaw.com/scripts/getcase.
pl?court=us&vol=365&invol=109
p. 51, par. 7; p. 55, par. 1, *Griffin* v. *Illinois*, 351 U.S. 12
(1956). http://caselaw.lp.findlaw.com/scripts/getcase.
pl?court=us&vol=351&invol=12

Sidebar

pp. 52–54, The Supreme Court Historical Society
http://www.supremecourthistory.org
Administrative Office of the U.S. Courts
http://www.uscourts.gov
Iowa Court Information System
http://www.judicial.state.ia.us/students/6
There is also a diagram on the last Web site.

Chapter 6

p. 58, par. 2, Brief for Petitioner, p. 22.
http://www.nacdl.org/public.nsf/GideonAnniversary/
pleadings?opendocument
p. 58, par. 3, Brief for Petitioner, p. 23.
p. 58, par. 6, Brief for Petitioner, p. 28.
p. 58, par. 7–p. 59, par. 1, Brief for Petitioner, p. 25.
p. 59, par. 3, Brief for Petitioner, p. 24.
p. 59, par. 5–p. 60, par. 1, Brief for Petitioner, p. 22.

p. 61, par. 2, Brief for Petitioner, p. 37.

p. 61, par. 5–p. 61, par. 1, Brief for Petitioner, p. 20.

p. 62, par. 3, Brief for Petitioner, p. 38.

p. 63, par. 3, Brief for Petitioner, p. 32.

p. 63, par. 4–p. 64, par. 1, Brief for Petitioner, p. 17.

p. 65, par. 1, Brief for Petitioner, p. 47.

p. 65, par. 1, Brief for Respondent, p. 7,
http://www.nacdl.org/public.nsf/GideonAnniversary/
pleadings?opendocument

p. 66, par. 4, Brief for Respondent, p. 30.

p. 66, par. 4, Brief for Respondent, p. 28.

p. 66, par. 6–p. 67, par. 1, Brief for Respondent, pp. 7–8.

p. 67, par. 2, Brief for Respondent, p. 28.

p. 67, par. 4, Brief for Respondent, p. 34.

p. 67, par. 5, Brief for Respondent, p. 8.

p. 68, par. 4–p. 69, par. 1, Brief for Respondent, p. 41.

p. 69, par. 2, Brief for Respondent, p. 40.

p. 69, par. 4–p. 70, par. 1, Brief for Respondent, p. 14.

p. 70, par. 3, Brief for Respondent, p. 19.

p. 70, par. 4, Brief for Respondent, p. 19.

p. 70, par. 5, Brief for Respondent, p. 7.

p. 71, par. 1, Brief for Respondent, p. 9.

p. 71, par. 3, Brief for Respondent, p. 10.

Chapter 7

p. 73, par. 1, Brief of State of Alabama as *Amicus Curiae*, p. 4.
http://www.nacdl.org/public.nsf/GideonAnniversary
/pleadings?opendocument

p. 73, par. 2, Brief of State of Alabama as *Amicus Curiae*,
p. 10.

p. 73, par. 3, Brief for Petitioner, p. 32. http://www.
nacdl.org/public.nsf/GideonAnniversary/pleadings?
opendocument

p. 73, par. 5–p. 74, par. 1, Brief of State of Alabama as
Amicus Curiae, p. 12.

p. 74, par. 3, Brief of State of Alabama as *Amicus Curiae*, p. 13.

p. 74, par. 5–p. 75, par. 1, Brief of State Governments (twenty-two states) as *Amicus Curiae*, p. 1. http://www.nacdl.org/public.nsf/GideonAnniversary/pleadings?opendocument

p. 75, par. 3, Brief of State Governments (twenty-two states) as *Amici Curiae*, p. 3.

p. 75, par. 4, Brief of State Governments (twenty-two states) as *Amici Curiae*, p. 21.

p. 75, par. 6, Brief of State Governments (twenty-two states) as *Amici Curiae*, pp. 24–25.

p. 76, par. 3, Brief of American Civil Liberties Union and the Florida Civil Liberties Union as *Amici Curiae*, pp. 47–50. http://www.nacdl.org/public nsf/Gideon Anniversary/pleadings?opendocument

p. 76, par. 5, Brief of American Civil Liberties Union and the Florida Civil Liberties Union as *Amici Curiae*, p. 18.

p. 76, par. 6; p. 78, par. 1, Brief of American Civil Liberties Union and the Florida Civil Liberties Union as *Amici Curiae*, p. 26.

p. 78, par. 2, Brief of American Civil Liberties Union and the Florida Civil Liberties Union as *Amici Curiae*, p. 26.

Chapter 8

p. 80, par. 4, Federal Court Concepts: The Supreme Court. Center for Assistive Technology and Environmental Access. Atlanta, Georgia. http://www.catea.org/grade/legal/scotus.html (Accessed January 5, 2006).

p. 81, par. 1, U.S. Supreme Court, "Guide for Counsel in Cases to Be Argued Before the Supreme Court of the United States." Supreme Court of the United States. October 2005, pp. 4–5. http://www.supremecourtus. gov/oral_arguments/oral_arguments.html

p. 81, par. 3, "Guide for Counsel," p. 5.

p. 81, par. 5, *Gideon* Oral Argument, January 15, 1963, http://www.rashkind.com/gideon/Gideon_v_%20 Wainwright_oral_argument_transcript.htm

p. 82, par. 2, *Gideon* Oral Argument.

p. 82, par. 4, *Gideon* Oral Argument.

p. 83, par. 2, *Gideon* Oral Argument.

p. 83, par. 4, *Gideon* Oral Argument.

p. 84, par. 1, Krash, Abe. "Architects of Gideon: Remembering Abe Fortas and Hugo Black." National Association of Criminal Defense Lawyers. March, 1998, http://www.nacdl.org/public.nsf/ChampionArticles/ 19980316?opendocument

p. 84, par. 2, *Gideon* Oral Argument.

p. 84, par. 3, *Gideon* Oral Argument.

p. 84, par. 7, *Gideon* Oral Argument.

p. 85, par. 2, *Gideon* Oral Argument.

p. 86, par. 3, *Gideon* Oral Argument.

p. 87, par. 7, *Gideon* Oral Argument.

p. 88, par. 1, *Gideon* Oral Argument.

p. 88, par. 3, *Gideon* Oral Argument.

p. 89, par. 1, *Gideon* Oral Argument.

p. 90, par. 2, *Gideon* Oral Argument.

p. 90, par. 3, *Gideon* Oral Argument.

Chapter 9

p. 93, par. 5, Sargent, Robert S. Jr., "Harry Blackmun and the Pursuit of Happiness." Enter Stage Right. March 15, 2004. http://www.enterstageright.com/archive/articles /0304/0304blackmunhappiness.htm

p. 96, par. 2, Newman, Roger K. *Hugo Black: A Biography*. New York: Pantheon Books, 1994, p. 528.

p. 97, par. 2, *Gideon v. Wainwright*, 372 U.S. 335 (1963). http://caselaw.lp.findlaw.com/scripts/getcase.pl?court =us&vol=372&invol=335

p. 97, par. 3, *Gideon* v. *Wainwright*, 372 U.S. 335 (1963).
p. 97, par. 6–p. 98, par. 1, *Gideon* v. *Wainwright*, 372 U.S. 335 (1963).
p. 98, par. 4, *Gideon* v. *Wainwright*, 372 U.S. 335 (1963).
p. 100, par. 1, *Gideon* v. *Wainwright*, 372 U.S. 335 (1963).
p. 101, par. 1, *Gideon* v. *Wainwright*, 372 U.S. 335 (1963).
p. 101, par. 3–p. 102, par. 1, *Gideon* v. *Wainwright*, 372 U.S. 335 (1963).
p. 102, par. 2, *Gideon* v. *Wainwright*, 372 U.S. 335 (1963).

Chapter 10
p. 105, par. 5, Editorial, *Washington Post*, August 11, 1963, p. E4.
p. 105, par. 6, Editorial, *St. Petersburg Times*, March 20, 1963, p. 14.
p. 107, par. 1, *Miranda* v. *Arizona*, 384 U.S. 436 (1966). Findlaw.com. http://laws.findlaw.com/us/384/436.html

Chapter 11
p. 109, par. 2, Lewis, Anthony. "The Silencing of Gideon's Trumpet." *New York Times Magazine*. April 20, 2003. http://www.deathpenaltyinfo.org/article.php?scid=17&did=595
p. 109, par. 4–p. 110, par. 1, Krash, Abe. "Architects of Gideon: Remembering Abe Fortas and Hugo Black." National Association of Criminal Defense Lawyers. March, 1998. http://www.nacdl.org/public.nsf/ChampionArticles/19980316?opendocument
p. 110, par. 3, Brief for Respondent, p. 10. http://www.nacdl.org/public.nsf/GideonAnniversary/pleadings?opendocument
p. 110, par. 6; p. 112, par. 1, Lewis, Anthony, "The Silencing of Gideon's Trumpet."
p. 112, par. 2, Lewis, "The Silencing of Gideon's Trumpet."

p. 112, par. 3, Jackson, Jesse L. Sr., Jesse L. Jackson Jr., and Bruce Shapiro. *Legal Lynching: The Death Penalty and America's Future.* New York: New Press, 2001, p. 36.

p. 112, par. 4, Brief for Petitioner, p. 35. http://www.nacdl.org/public.nsf/GideonAnniversary/ pleadings?opendocument

p. 113, par.2, Taylor-Thompson, Kim. "Tuning Up Gideon's Trumpet." *Fordham Law Review*, March 2003. http://research.umbc.edu/~davisj/gideon.html

p. 113, par. 5, Taylor-Thompson, "Tuning Up."

p. 114, par. 2, Leahy, William J. "A Somber Birthday." Committee for Public Counsel Services. http://www.mass.gov/cpcs/Gideon_ %20Remarks.htm (Accessed January 7, 2006.)

p. 114, par. 4, Pratt, Mary K. "Court-appointed Lawyers Seek Boost in Compensation." *Boston Business Journal*, March 8, 2004. http://boston.bizjournals.com/ boston/stories/2004/03/08/focus14.html

p. 115, par. 1, Brewer, Steve and Mike Tolson. "Court-appointed defense: Critics charge the system is unfair." *Houston Chronicle.* http://www.chron.com/cs/CDA/ ssistory.mpl/special/penalty/816535 (Accessed December 12, 2005.)

p. 115, par. 3, Taylor-Thompson, "Tuning Up."

Chapter 12
p. 116, par. 1, *Gideon v. Wainwright*, 372 U.S. 335 (1963). http://caselaw.lp.findlaw.com/scripts/getcase.pl?court =us&vol=372&invol=335

p. 117, par. 3, Lewis, Anthony. "The Silencing of Gideon's Trumpet." *New York Times Magazine.* April 20, 2003. http://www.deathpenaltyinfo.org/article.php?scid=17& did=595

p. 118, par. 5, Lewis, Anthony, "The Silencing of Gideon's Trumpet."

p. 121, par. 2, *Gideon* Oral Argument, January 15, 1963.
http://www.rashkind.com/gideon/Gideon_v_%20
Wainwright_oral_argument_transcript.htm

p. 121, par. 4, Krash, Abe. "Architects of Gideon:
Remembering Abe Fortas and Hugo Black." National
Association of Criminal Defense Lawyers. March, 1998.
http://www.nacdl.org/public.nsf/ChampionArticles/
19980316?opendocument

p. 123, par. 2, Ritchie, Robert W. "The Defense of the
Accused: Past, Present and Future," December 16, 2003.
http://www.rfdlaw.com/defaccused.html

p. 123, par. 3, National Association of Criminal Defense
Lawyers. http://www.nacdl.org/public.nsf/Gideon
Anniversary/Index1/$FILE/GideonGrave.jpg (Accessed
January 5, 2006.)

All Internet sites accessible as of March 15, 2006.

FurtHer information

FURTHER READING
Haskins, James. *The Scottsboro Boys*. New York: Holt, 1993.

Kowalski, Kathiann M. *Order in the Court: A Look at the Judicial Branch*. Minneapolis, MN: Lerner Publications, 2004.

McKissack, Pat. *To Establish Justice: Citizenship and the Constitution*. New York: Knopf, 2004.

Morin, Isobel V. *Our Changing Constitution: How and Why We Have Amended It*. Brookfield, CT: Millbrook Press, 1998.

The Oxford Companion to the Supreme Court of the United States. New York: Oxford University Press, 1992.

Sherrow, Victoria. Gideon v. Wainwright: *Free Legal Counsel*. Berkeley Heights, NJ: Enslow Publishers, 1995.

WEB SITES
These Web sites are good places to pick up information
and ideas on the issues discussed in this book.

Findlaw.com
http://www.findlaw.com/casecode/supreme.html
Free, easy-to-search database of U.S. Supreme Court
opinions dating back to 1893.

Landmark Supreme Court Cases
http://www.landmarkcases.org/gideon/background3.html
A site developed for teachers and students, featuring
documents relating to *Gideon* v. *Wainwright* as well as
commentary and thought-provoking questions.

The 'Lectric Law Library *Lawcopedia*'s Constitutional Law
& Rights Topic Area
http://www.lectlaw.com/tcon.htm
Information on a wide variety of legal issues connected
with constitutional rights.

National Association of Criminal Defense Lawyers:
Gideon at 40: Fulfilling the Promise
http://www.nacdl.org/gideon
This comprehensive site dedicated to *Gideon* v. *Wainwright*
includes all the court documents relating to the case and
many articles and speeches commenting on the case.

The U.S. Constitution Online
http://www.usconstitution.net
This site, aimed at young people, gives an in-depth look
at the Constitution, the Bill of Rights, the Declaration of
Independence, and some state constitutions. Includes
frequently asked questions, a timeline, and a section on
the Miranda warning.

United States Supreme Court
http://www.supremecourtus.gov
Official site of the nation's highest court, packed with
information on the history of the Court, how the Court
works, and its current cases.

BIBLIOGraPHY

BOOKS
Lewis, Anthony. *Gideon's Trumpet*. New York: Random House, 1964.

Newman, Roger K. *Hugo Black. A Biography*. New York: Pantheon Books, 1994.

Gideon **DOCUMENTS**
Brief for Petitioner
Brief for Respondent
Brief of American Civil Liberties Union and Florida Civil Liberties Union as Amici Curiae
Brief of State Governments (twenty-two states) as Amici Curiae
Brief of State of Alabama as Amicus Curiae
Florida's Response to Petition for Writ of Certiorari
Gideon's Answer to Response for Petition for Writ of Certiorari
Gideon's Motion to Proceed in Forma Pauperis and Petition for Writ of Certiorari
Oral Argument, January 15, 1963

All of above available at http://www.nacdl.org/public.nsf/ GideonAnniversary/pleadings?opendocument

U.S. Supreme Court Ruling: *Gideon* v. *Wainwright*, 372 U.S. 335 (1963) http://caselaw.lp.findlaw.com/scripts/getcase.pl?court=us&vol=372&invol=335

RELATED CASES

Betts v. *Brady*, 316 U.S. 455 (1942)

Brown v. *Board of Education*, 347 U.S. 483 (1954)

Gallegos v. *Nebraska*, 342 U.S. 55 (1951)

Griffin v. *Illinois*, 351 U.S. 12 (1956) 351 U.S. 12

Johnson v. *Zerbst*, 304 U.S. 458 (1938)

McNeal v. *Culver*, 365 U.S. 109 (1961)

Miranda v. *Arizona*, 384 U.S. 436 (1966)

Plessy v. *Ferguson*, 163 U.S. 537 (1896)

Powell v. *State of Alabama*, 287 U.S. 45 (1932)

Uveges v. *Commonwealth of Pennsylvania*, 335 U.S. 437 (1948)

index

Page numbers in **boldface** are illustrations, tables, and charts.

about the author

RON FRIDELL has written for radio, television, newspapers, and textbooks. He has written books on social and political issues, such as terrorism and espionage, and scientific topics, such as DNA fingerprinting and global warming. His most recent book for Marshall Cavendish Benchmark was *Miranda Law: The Right to Remain Silent*, in our Supreme Court series. He taught English as a second language while a member of the Peace Corps in Bangkok, Thailand. He lives in Florida with his wife Patricia and his dog, an Australian shepherd named Madeline.